WITHDRAWN

Gender and Land Reform

Gender and Land Reform

The Zimbabwe Experience

A L L I S O N G O E B E L

McGill-Queen's University Press
Montreal & Kingston · London · Ithaca

© McGill-Queen's University Press 2005
ISBN 0-7735-2842-3

Legal deposit second quarter 2005
Bibliothèque nationale du Québec

Printed in Canada on acid-free paper that is 100%
ancient forest free (100% post-consumer recycled),
processed chlorine free.

This book has been published with the help of a grant
from the Canadian Federation for the Humanities
and Social Sciences, through the Aid to Scholarly
Publications Programme, using funds provided by the
Social Sciences and Humanities Research Council
of Canada.

McGill-Queen's University Press acknowledges the
support of the Canada Council for the Arts for our
publishing program. We also acknowledge the
financial support of the Government of Canada
through the Book Publishing Industry Development
Program (BPIDP) for our publishing activities.

**Library and Archives Canada Cataloguing
in Publication**

Goebel, Allison, 1963–
    Gender and land reform : the Zimbabwe experience /
    Allison Goebel.
    Includes bibliographical references and index.
    ISBN 0-7735-2842-3
    1. Land reform – Zimbabwe. 2. Women's rights –
    Zimbabwe. 3. Women in agriculture – Zimbabwe –
    Social conditions. 4. Land settlement – Government
    policy – Zimbabwe. I. Title.
    HD1333.Z55G63 2005   333.3′16891   C2004-904804-X

Typeset in Palatino 10/13
by Caractéra inc., Quebec City

Contents

Figure and Table

Abbreviations

AIDS acquired immunodeficiency syndrome
CA communal area
ESAP Economic Structural Adjustment Program
GAD gender and development
GMB Grain Marketing Board
HIV human immunodeficiency virus
LAMA Legal Age of Majority Act
MDC Movement for Democratic Change
NLHA Native Land Husbandry Act
NRB Natural Resources Board
PRA participatory rural appraisal
RA resettlement area
RO resettlement officer
TTL Tribal Trust Lands
VIDCO Village Development Committee
WAG Women's Action Group
WARDCO Ward Development Committee
WLLG Women and Land Lobby Group
WLSA Women and Law in Southern Africa Research Trust
ZINATHA Zimbabwe Traditional Healers Association
ZRP Zimbabwe Republic Police
ZWRCN Zimbabwe Women's Resource Centre and Network

Acknowledgments

In Zimbabwe, the farmers of the Sengezi Resettlement in Wedza District deserve special thanks for their hospitality and generosity during my field research in their country. Nyaradzo Dzobo (Mrs Shayanewako) and Charles Shayanewako and their children, Simba and Wadzanai, offered me their home in Sengezi, and this research would not have been possible without them. Mrs Shayanewako also became my chief field assistant and dear friend. Moses Goto, Mujeyi Tizora, Stella Chipenzi, Doreen Chinzou, Estery Kwaramba, and Henrietta Shayanewako served as field assistants for much of the field research. Scholars at the University of Zimbabwe, especially Bruce Campbell, Alois Mandondo, Billy Mukamuri, Nontokozo Nabane, Calvin Nhira, Joseph Mutambirwa, and Bev Sithole, offered invaluable feedback and advice throughout my field research. Mr Mandondo also translated most of my interview questionnaires from English to Shona. Solomon Chirere of the Institute of Environmental Studies provided technical assistance and company on our many drives to and from Sengezi. Mr Kanotunga, the resettlement officer of Sengezi at that time, offered me accommodation and many interviews during the research period. I would like to thank Abby Mgugu of the Women and Land Lobby Group in Zimbabwe, who took the time to explain the WLLG's vision and actions and who generously shared WLLG and government documents when I was in Harare in 2002.

In North America, Dr Susan McDaniel and Dr Eloise Murray of the University of Alberta were stellar in their supervision and support for the PHD portion of this project. Dr Louise Fortmann of Berkeley offered important advice in her role as external examiner of the PHD thesis, much of which I have incorporated in the writing of this book. The International Development Research Centre of Canada (IDRC) financially supported most of this fieldwork through the Value of Trees Project and the Young Canadian Researcher's Award. Financial support was also given by the Social Science and Humanities Research Council of Canada (SSHRC) and the University of Alberta. Queen's University financially supported my field trip in 2002 and the writing of the manuscript.

Finally, the unflagging love, support, editing talent, and prodigious knowledge of my partner, Marc Epprecht, and the love, patience, and adventurous spirits of our three children, Jenn, Adriane, and Gabriel, made it all happen.

Some of the material presented in chapters 3, 4, and 5 has been published in an earlier and abbreviated article form in "'Here it is our land, the two of us': Women, Men and Land in a Zimbabwean Resettlement Area," *Journal of Contemporary African Studies* 17 (1) (1999). Some sections of chapter 6 appear in somewhat different form in "Gender, Environment and Development in Southern Africa," *Canadian Journal of Development Studies* 23 (2) (2002), and "Gender and Entitlements in the Zimbabwean Woodlands: A Case Study of Resettlement," in Patricia Howard-Borjas, ed., *Women and Plants: Case Studies on Gender Relations in Local Plant Genetic Resource Management* (Zed Books, 2003). A different version of chapter 7 appears in *Canadian Journal of African Studies* 36 (3) (2002), and various sections throughout the book inform a forthcoming article in 2005 in *Gender, Place and Culture*.

I would like to thank the anonymous reviewers and McGill-Queen's University Press for their advice and help in preparing the manuscript for publication.

Gender and Land Reform

1 Departure Points

"Land issue a time bomb"

INTRODUCTION

The issue of land reform in Zimbabwe has captured worldwide attention since the year 2000, when mass land occupations firmly punctuated a growing political and economic crisis. By contrast, little attention has been given, in either scholarly or popular writing, to the gendered contours of the land issue in Zimbabwe. This book inserts consideration of women's situation and gender relations within the context of the political and economic issues in the land reform process, with particular focus on the resettlement program of the 1980s and 1990s, but includes as well a discussion of the implications for women and gender of the more recent "fast track" land reform process that has come out of the occupations of the late 1990s. The conditions under which people have been allocated resettlement land and the ways they use (and sometimes lose) it provide a central site for the creation of gender relations. Women and men's relationships to agricultural land are fundamentally different, and these differences can have deep consequences for women's status, standard of living, and survival. Additionally, the resettlement program in Zimbabwe has had important effects on household structure and dynamics with ramifications for gender relations.

To date, women's perspectives and needs have been marginalized by the state and its advisers in land reform. Nevertheless, Zimbabwe's post-independence resettlement program involved important improvements in some women's relationships to land and more cooperation within marriages. These improvements, however, have come with ideological and cultural struggle and exist within an over-all context of vulnerability and danger for women. This book details these dynamic gender relations and struggles through a case study of the Sengezi Resettlement in east-central Zimbabwe. In particular, this study examines the different forces and effects in the resettlement process, from the level of state policy and relevant legislation, through customary norms and practices, through local institutions, ideologies and cosmologies, household structures, and people's prac-tices. The study also provides an opportunity to examine the strategic moves women make in new institutional and household contexts. Especially important is the identification of the kinds of opportunities that afford women room to manoeuvre, the aspects of the rural and household economies where their control is fairly robust, and the forms and locations that opposition to women's interests takes as women struggle for change. Throughout the book, women's voices and perspectives are foregrounded in a way that I hope brings their struggles alive for readers and affords participants in this study the dignity they strongly deserve.

This study is important in a number of ways. First, very little academic work has been done on women and land resettlement in Zimbabwe. Susie Jacobs's mid-1980s study offers important depar-ture points but requires updating (Jacobs 1984, 1991, 1992), while Chenaux-Repond's (1993) work offers an important, but narrow, focus on the gendered implications and flaws in the permit system. This study hence fills a void by providing a comprehensive exami-nation of gender issues in the resettlement process in the late 1990s. In so doing, this work sheds light on the trajectories of the current struggles for land in Zimbabwe's political and economic crisis. Sec-ond, the land reform process in Zimbabwe defines the country's nationalist ambitions and achievements like no other issue. Land reform goes to the very heart of what was dreamed for an indepen-dent Zimbabwe and is therefore of critical interest to peasant and revolutionary studies worldwide. This book assesses Zimbabwe's successes and failures in inserting issues of gender justice within the broader project of land redistribution.

The remainder of this first chapter provides background to the land reform process in Zimbabwe more generally, as located in the colonial and post-colonial history of land distribution, and to the current political and economic crisis. Chapter 2 inserts the question of gender into the "land question" in Zimbabwe within historical and contemporary contexts and analyses the central role of the state in understanding women's relationships to land. The chapter also discusses the salience of gender and focuses on women more broadly in Zimbabwe, addressing key feminist theoretical concerns and empirical studies. A description of the case study site and the methodology of the study are also included.

Chapter 3 discusses the central place of marriage in determining women's relationship to resettlement land, in terms of both how women are treated under resettlement policy and how they are treated as wives in households. Accordingly, feminist theoretical concepts of households are considered as tools in analysing these dynamics. The chapter also looks at the gendered dynamics of crop production and income generation for married women. Evidence in this chapter illuminates ways in which the state is patriarchal and conservative in regard to women's initial access to resettlement land, but also how, despite this, women are grasping economic opportunities that emerge in a context of relative land abundance.

Chapter 4 continues the discussion of married women's situations by documenting some of the ways in which state agents in resettlement have treated married women as farmers in their own right, hence improving women's status as farmers and their economic opportunities and leverage within households. Interlinked with this are the effects of the resettlement process on household structures and internal dynamics, including rates of polygyny, extended family relationships, gendered economic responsibility, and decision making. The data presented in this chapter reveal the importance of a nuanced analysis of the effects of the state and its agents on women's experiences.

Chapter 5 examines the experiences of widows and divorcees. As unattached women, they have profoundly different experiences than married women. Resettlement policy treats them differently, in some cases providing new opportunities for access to land and resisting cultural practices that the women view as against their interest, and in other cases creating conditions leading to destitution and landlessness. The personal stories of widows and divorcees in this chapter provide powerful testimony both to women's strength and perseverance and to their vulnerability to injustice.

Chapter 6 outlines the local institutional context and its implications for women's relationships to resettlement land. Village Development Committees (VIDCOS), which are the local state institutions, and "traditional" institutions and practices are discussed. In both cases, the institutions are seen to operate in ways that undermine women's claims to resettlement land in their own right. Local state institutions marginalize women as political actors, while traditional institutions operate within a cultural logic that is deeply patriarchal and patrilocal, having the effect of distancing women from land rights. Chapter 6 also argues for the usefulness of a feminist political-ecology approach in understanding the institutional, political, and cultural elements of women's relationship to land and in understanding this relationship more broadly as part of the total social system of human/environment relations.

Chapter 7 narrows the focus to the micro-relations of gender in households by investigating the social phenomenon of husband-taming herbs. Study of the widespread use of herbs and regimes by women to control their errant husbands illuminates key aspects of current gender relations, such as marital instability and women's consequent desperation, the effects of the HIV/AIDS pandemic, the role of traditional healers in marital problems, and the active transformation of cultural institutions and ideologies in new contexts. This chapter is important in that it illustrates that while the larger structural context of state policy and cultural practices is crucial to an understanding of women's situations and experiences, for the women themselves, a major aspect of their battle occurs at home.

Chapter 8 provides a conclusion to the book and looks ahead to the implications for women and gender relations of the current and future land reform process.

"LAND ISSUE A TIME BOMB"[1]

Through a brief history of land use and allocation, this section illustrates three main points about the land question in post-colonial Zimbabwe. First, it emphasizes the pressing historical legacy of racial injustice in regard to land distribution. Second, and more subtly, the account identifies continuities in Zimbabwe's post-independence land reform process with the colonial past. These continuities help explain the difficulties of realizing the revolutionary vision of the war of liberation, which included massive land redistribution to the rural poor. Finally, this account identifies the class-based interests of the emergent African elite in post-independence Zimbabwe as a major factor in pushing the agenda of land reform towards an increasingly exclusionary process emphasizing the transfer of land from white elites to black elites.

Zimbabwe is a former British colony in Southern Africa that was previously known as Southern Rhodesia and then Rhodesia. The British South Africa Company, under the leadership of Cecil Rhodes, originally penetrated the area in search of mineral wealth in the late nineteenth century. While the hoped-for gold did not materialize, the area was soon valued for its agricultural potential. Like Kenya, it became an important white settler colony in the early twentieth century. A protracted and bloody guerrilla war finally led to a negotiated handover of political power under the Lancaster House Agreement in 1979, freeing black Zimbabweans from white settler rule.

Zimbabwe's colonial past was marked by profound land inequities, with white settlers controlling the greater part of the most fertile land. The colonial government of Southern Rhodesia formally demarcated land into "Native" (African)* and "European" areas through the Land Apportionment Act of 1930. Indigenous farmers were sometimes forced to move from their land to make way for white farmers. Moreover, the sandy soils originally occupied by indigenous farmers (as they suited African agricultural practices of the time) became infertile and eroded under conditions of land scarcity (because of white control of much of the land) and population growth throughout the twentieth century. For the majority of black peasant farmers, the African "reserves," called Tribal Trust Lands (TTLS), became an insufficient base for subsistence, a symbol for racial injustice, and the focus of a rallying cry for nationalist resistance (Bourdillon 1987; Cheater 1990; Moyana 1984; Moyo 1986, 2000; Palmer 1977; Bhebe and Ranger 1995).

The division of land in Southern Rhodesia into African and European areas through the Land Apportionment Act of 1930 was defined by different tenure regimes as well as by racial categories. European land was designated as private property, with title deeds and inheritance laws in keeping with Roman Dutch Law, which applied to the settler

---

* The word "Native" was used by colonial officials but carries a negative connotation among black Africans in Zimbabwe. It is used in this text only for historical accuracy.

population. Land tenure in African areas, the reserves, was based on a colonial understanding or construction of "traditional" African landholding systems. Although there was evidence of buying and selling of land among Africans in the region, the colonial government preferred to construct African landholding as "communal." With the 1930 act, practices in the reserves were formalized. Africans were to be granted usufruct rights by their chief, who held the land in trust for the state. In practice, however, the authority to allocate land seemed to fall primarily to the Native commissioner, and the ultimate ownership of the land by the state meant that people could be relocated through the directive of the state (Moyana 1984: 13; Cheater 1990). Grazing and woodland areas were used as common property resources, while homesteads and fields tended to stay within a family. The buying up of large tracts of land by "reserve entrepreneurs," whose activities had worried colonial officials, was outlawed in the reserves. Reserves had to be maintained as a "social security net" for all Africans (Shutt 1995).

The Land Apportionment Act of 1930 also created Native purchase areas (areas where Africans were able to buy title to small-scale farms) to cater to African demand for larger tracks of land. Before 1930, Africans technically held the right to own land, and the Morris Carter Commission of 1925 identified a small number of African landholders, mostly originating from South Africa. White settlers were nervous about this as well as about reserve entrepreneurs. By providing purchase areas for Africans, the 1930 act regulated African land purchase, hence protecting European land dominance while providing an outlet for aspiring and successful African farmers. As it turned out, purchase areas also attracted urban and mission dwellers, and the farmers, whose numbers remained small, nevertheless "became, in effect, a rural middle-class" (Shutt 1995: xiv).

Over the colonial decades and continuing into the post-colonial era, land use and allocation practices in African areas strayed from the colonial codification of "communal tenure." There is a long history of squatting and self-allocation both in reserves (which became communal areas after independence in 1980) and in the post-independence resettlement areas (Nyambara 2001; D.S. Moore 1993; Hughes 1999). This history challenges a notion of a consistent and neatly practised system of communal land tenure and instead points to messiness, irregularities, and negotiation in land allocation in African areas. In addition, chiefs and headmen continued to allocate land in communal areas after 1980 despite the formal loss of those powers under the new government (Andersson 1999; Goebel and Nabane 1998). Hughes (1999) notes that in Eastern Zimbabwe the headman even allocated land to refugees from Mozambique, while Rutherford (2001b) discusses the allocation of communal area homesteads and fields to foreign-born commercial farm workers or their descendants in the Hurungwe area. Furthermore, post-colonial state-led land use practices such as those under CAMPFIRE (Communal Management Programme for Indigenous Resources) in some cases impose new restrictions on communal tenure and entitlements (Dzingirai 2003; Hughes 2001). Hence, an account of the history of land in Zimbabwe must avoid the deployment of a rigid and generalized notion of communal and subsistence land use practices in African areas.

The views on land use of early settler governments in the first decades of the twentieth century were also marked by environmental concerns. Originally, colonial officials feared that the destructive mining and farming practices of white settlers would cause rapid deforestation, river siltation, and soil exhaustion (Elliott 1991; Grove 1989; McGregor 1995; Beinart 1984, 1989). These concerns were also raised in other colonies of Southern Africa and in India, Australia, and the United States, reflecting a scientific discourse of the time that predicted rapid deforestation and desertification (Beinart 1984; Grove 1989).

Colonial governments in Southern Africa responded to the perceived crisis by developing rational-technical approaches to conservation. These initially were directed at white commercial farmers in the interest of saving a future for capitalist farming in the region (Beinart 1984). In the 1920s, the colonial concern for conservation increasingly included African areas. Some officials argued that African farmers caused more destruction than Europeans (McGregor 1995). In 1927, E.D. Alvord, then a senior technical assistant in the agricultural department, undertook the first serious efforts to improve African agriculture by sending African agricultural demonstrators to the reserves. Using demonstration plots with "cooperating" farmers, the department initiated the Master Farmer Certificate system, wherein farmers undertaking the "modern" methods were issued with certificates. The first such certificate was issued in 1933. By 1944, 174 had been issued (Southern Rhodesia 1944: 22–3). Besides promoting certain farming practices, beginning in 1929 in Rhodesia, the interventions included efforts towards centralization, which rationalized African areas by designating planned-settlement, arable, and grazing areas. In addition, in the 1930s and 1940s, African farmers, who were thought of as "careless and dangerous to the environment" (Beinart 1984: 61), were instructed to preserve forests and stream banks, to fill in erosion ditches, but, mostly, to improve tillage practices, destock, and dig contour ridges (Beinart 1984; McGregor 1995). The new methods were about development but also about conservation (Beinart 1984, 1989; Drinkwater 1989; McGregor 1995; Wilson 1995). The approach included elements of social Darwinist thinking that cast Africans as unscientific and backward, making it difficult for officials to see indigenous practices as purposefully ecological (Beinart 1989). The following quotations from the *Report of Native Production and Trade Commission* (Southern Rhodesia 1944) give some sense of colonial thinking on the nature of the African as farmer:

The male Native in the Reserves appears to suffer from an extraordinary form of lethargy ... a large number of male adult Natives in the Reserves seem to be without desire to improve their conditions of life and appear to be content to continue to live under existing conditions ... The task of the Government and the officials of the Native Department ... is therefore no easy one in their endeavours to bring him slowly and surely – there is no short-cut – to understand, appreciate and practise our ideas of civilization and to realize that whatever is done for him cannot be of lasting benefit without considerable effort on his part. (P. 7)

[I]rresponsibility and indiscipline were prevalent among Natives ... practical measures to remove or diminish these undesirable features became a major issue of our inquiry. (P. 10)

[F]orward peoples while preserving their settled economy have a duty by all reasonable and proper means to assist backward peoples to progress and for that purpose to enforce discipline without oppression ... it is the duty of backward peoples to contribute to their own advancement to the limit of their powers and to observe proper discipline. (P. 10)

Colonial views were not, of course, homogeneous. Both Elliott (1991) and Beinart (1984) uncover the objection of some officials, particularly those working directly with African farmers, to labelling Africans destructive and "ignorant." In 1929 the Native commissioner for Marandellas lamented the loss of indigenous knowledge caused by European educational programs (Elliott 1991: 79), while others pointed out that African practices were far less destructive than those used by the white settlers. In fact, rather than being thought of as inherently destructive, African practices were more likely considered problematic in the new context of intensive agriculture created by the settling of Africans permanently in the reserves. Prior to this, the shifting slash-and-burn agricultural practices were not thought to do permanent damage, as land was left to regenerate (Southern Rhodesia 1944: 21–2).

Despite such conciliatory opinions, dominant views tended to see African practices as environmentally problematic. Practices such as the leaving of trees in arable fields were understood not as part of traditional environmental management, but as signs of backwardness and laziness (Wilson 1989). The focus on peasant practices and ignorance in environmental management also provided an ideological context where the injustice of land segregation was a non-issue. African development meant technical improvement and modernization of practices. This official approach to African agriculture culminated in the Native Land Husbandry Act of 1951, which attempted a form of privatization of African landholdings and enforced strict conservationist methods in farming (Elliott 1991). The Native Land Husbandry Act states its overall purpose as follows: "To provide for the control of the utilisation and allocation of land occupied by natives and to ensure its efficient use for agricultural purposes; to require natives to perform labour for conserving natural resources and for promoting good land husbandry"(Southern Rhodesia 1952: 893). Implementation of this act had to be abandoned owing to extensive resistance. It is often held that, more than any other factor, resistance to these impositions, particularly destocking, solidified peasant support for the guerrilla movement that eventually liberated Zimbabwe from white rule (Moyana 1984; Ranger 1985).[2]

Throughout the 1960s and 1970s the Rhodesian government continued its efforts to increase agricultural productivity in the Tribal Trust Lands, or reserves, through irrigation schemes, improved access to credit, and other interventions. The Tribal Trust Lands Act of 1967 fixed boundaries for the TTLS, and the Land Tenure Act of 1969 confirmed this distribution and attempted to improve land use and conservation by enforcing rules on stock limitation and land management. The Land Husbandry Act of 1970 provided for the use of traditional leaders in the supervision of conservation, an arrangement that had implications for the dynamics of local leadership vis-à-vis the guerrillas in the 1970s (Nkala 1996: 63–4). However, the state's efforts in the 1960s and 1970s to "improve" African agriculture and conservation practices largely failed because of the increased disturbances of the bush war (Wekwete 1991; Zinyama 1991). The language used to describe African peasant farmers in documents from the 1970s is much tamer than that of earlier times, but the analysis remains the same: the only hope for African farming is to modernize methods through a system of rural improvement and identification and support for "progressive" farmers. For example, the *Agricultural Development Authority Rhodesia: Annual Report and Accounts* (1973) presents the following position: "The Authority believes that certain groups of tribesmen are willing to subject themselves to self-control in order to obtain the development required to institute properly managed economic schemes" (Rhodesia 1973: 9).

The Rural Land Act of 1979 provided the legal basis for the establishment of resettlement areas (Nkala 1996: 53). Further, the transition government of Zimbabwe-Rhodesia published a development plan in 1979 (Zimbabwe-Rhodesia 1979) that included a resettlement plan designed to relieve some of the pressure on the Tribal Trust Lands while not disturbing the commercial sector. It proposed the resettlement of 10,100 "good farming" families on 4.1 million hectares of underutilized commercial farming land (i.e., about 27 per cent of commercial farming land) over a ten-year period. The plan rejected large-scale resettlement, as it would threaten commercial agriculture, which was central to the economy, and would "extend the deterioration of the present tribal trust lands across the whole country" (Zimbabwe-Rhodesia 1979: 2). The most important planks in the plan for the development of African rural areas, the document suggested, were the improvement of basic services and practices in the reserves and relief of population pressure. Many of those farming in the reserves were not "real" farmers, the plan claimed, but people who had nowhere else to go. Hence, the plan argued, job creation and urbanization were the keys to relieving the resource base in the reserves. The overall most important aspect of agricultural development, the plan suggested, was support of the commercial farming sector, which earned about half of the country's foreign exchange and employed 38 per cent of wage-earning Africans.

THE POST-INDEPENDENCE CONTEXT

In the early years of post-independence Zimbabwe, the critical views of the Liberation War set the tone for government analysis of land degradation in the African sector. In this view, land degradation resulted from the unjust land distribution policy of the colonialists, wherein peasants were forced off the most fertile land and compelled to adopt unsustainable practices on account of the land shortage. The remedy was large-scale land redistribution and resettlement. The *Transitional National Development Plan 1982/83–1984/85* spoke of the "opportunity to create a new order, to rid the Zimbabwean society of vestiges of exploitation, unemployment, poverty, disease, ignorance and social insecurity" (Zimbabwe 1982: 1). The opening remarks included the view that "[r]esettlement of landless people in areas where they can make a decent living is a priority and must be implemented urgently if the unity of the nation is to be sustained" (Zimbabwe 1982: 2). The plan pointed out that 6,000 mostly white commercial farmers owned 44 per cent of the total land in Zimbabwe, mostly in the three best agro-ecological zones, while 700,000 African families occupied 42 per cent of the land. This land was in poorer zones and had a "carrying capacity" of less than half the current numbers (see Palmer 1977). The African areas suffered severe soil erosion caused by population pressure, poor services, and poor land husbandry. Half of the rural people owned no cattle for draught power, and one-fifth had no rights to land. The government's first objective for rural and agricultural development was hence an acceptable and fair distribution of landownership and land use. Its number-one strategy to achieve this, according to the plan, was a land resettlement program. The government planned to spend $260 million over the plan period to settle 162,000 families on 4.2 million hectares of unused and 3 million hectares of underutilized commercial land. Recognizing the need to protect the interests of commercial farming, the plan suggested that land currently out of serious commercial production be used. Also recognizing the limits of resettlement in dealing with the problems of population pressure and resource exhaustion in the reserves (now communal areas), the plan included large-scale improvements in the communal areas:

The resettlement programme will go some way towards redressing inequities in land distribution and relieving some of the population pressure in the Communal Areas. However, this programme by itself will not provide a lasting solution to the problem posed by a rapidly growing population and finite land supply ... Therefore measures will be taken to improve productivity in Communal Lands, generate maximum off-farm employment and increase levels of employment in the industrial sector. (Zimbabwe 1982: 61)

The plan advocated environmentally sound land management in the communal areas through the implementation of "technical measures and education of people to increase their consciousness of the importance of conserving our land resources" (Zimbabwe 1982: 61).

The approach of the early post-independence government clearly shared many similarities with the colonial and transitional government approaches (see Alexander 1994: 331–2). Emphasis was laid on modernizing farming practices in peasant areas and increasing awareness and practices of environmentally sound land use systems. The major difference was the emphasis on resettlement. The new government envisioned settling 162,000 families in the first five years of independence, while the transitional government had suggested only 10,100 over a period of ten years. Also, the post-independence government emphasized meeting the needs of the landless, while the transitional government had urged that settlers be "good farming families."

The early resettlement program of the 1980s proposed four types of resettlement models. Model A, Normal Intensive Resettlement, was the most common and is similar in structure to communal lands: families are settled in nucleated villages and given permits to reside there and cultivate and depasture stock. Grazing and bush areas are treated as the common property of all who fall within the village boundaries. As with all resettlement models, landownership lies with the state, which has ultimate authority over land use practices and the selection of settlers. A resettlement officer and an agricultural extension worker live on the site, the former to oversee the following of resettlement rules and to settle disputes (such as over succession to the permits) and the latter to train and oversee the farmers' practice of modern agricultural methods. This model would later include the Accelerated Intensive Resettlement model, designed to deal with the problem of squatters on former commercial farms. This model follows Model A structures but includes a minimum of infrastructure and service development so that squatters' land use can be formalized more quickly. Model B is a cooperative model wherein groups of between fifty and two hundred members live and farm cooperatively. Model C settles farmers through a lease system on state-owned estates, such as tobacco, coffee, or dairy, and farmers benefit from state infrastructure, such as processing or marketing facilities. Model D is a grazing scheme rather than a resettlement model. Of these models, Model A has dominated and Model B has been declared a failure.[3] The scheme focused on for most of this book, the Sengezi Resettlement in Wedza

District, is of the original Normal Intensive Model A type and in 1981 was one of the first to be established in the country.

From the beginning, however, resettlement was hampered by the government's conciliatory approach to the transition of power. Having to obtain land under the Lancaster House Agreement (1979) limited the government to willing seller/buyer deals. Although London pledged economic support for land purchase, Zimbabwe was required to come up with the money first, in hard currency, which would then be reimbursed (Alexander 1994; Zinyama 1991; Wekwete 1991; Cliffe 1988b). White commercial farmers were quick to take advantage of the government's desire to purchase land, selling off their least productive lands at high prices and thereby increasing their own efficiency and profitability (Munslow 1985: 45). By 1984 only 28,600 families had been resettled.

Resettlement also faced bureaucratic instability. In 1980 the Ministry of Lands, Resettlement and Rural Development was formed, giving resettlement a high profile. However, its activities soon became squeezed by the older ministries of Agriculture and Local Government and Town Planning, and hampered by its dependence on the technical expertise lodged in the Ministry of Agriculture. In 1985 the Ministry of Lands, Resettlement and Rural Development was dissolved, and its responsibilities were divided between the two older ministries, seriously reducing the profile for resettlement (Wekwete 1991). In another bureaucratic shift in the 1990s, resettlement became housed within the Ministry of Lands and Water Development in the Department of Rural Development (DERUDE). Changes in government structures at the district level have also affected resettlement. In 1993 the Rural District Council Act of 1988 was implemented, amalgamating the district councils (DCs) and rural district councils (RDCs). Prior to this, resettlement fell under the jurisdiction of the DC, as did the communal areas, while the RDC administered the commercial farms. This dual structure was a legacy of white rule, wherein African and European areas were administered separately.[4] Although resettlement technically fell under the DC before 1993, such activities as the maintenance of roads and the development of schools were the responsibility of the resettlement authority, while such responsibilities in neighbouring communal areas fell to the DC. In practice, this bred confusion and inefficiency.[5] In the mid-1990s, twenty-five ministries, departments, or parastatals had a role in resettlement (Lopes 1996: 23).

From the outset, the new government recognized the importance of white commercial farming for a large portion of the country's domestic food production and export earnings (Zimbabwe 1982). Its original resettlement plan had intended to respect this by only using land not currently under full use by commercial farmers. However, throughout the 1980s, the government bowed further to commercial farmer interests and delayed in demarcating much of the land it had previously stated was underutilized (Drinkwater 1989; Elliott 1991; Jacobs 1991; Zinyama 1991; Wekwete 1991). This was partly due to external macro-economic and political pressures. The worldwide economic recession of the early 1980s led to a rapid decline in annual economic growth rates in Zimbabwe and pressures from the United States and Britain not to disturb the economic contribution of commercial farming. These pressures were part of a wider tendency in the donor community not to include land reform in its conception of development in Zimbabwe; the donor community instead supported efforts to improve practices in the existing land distribution context (Moyo 1996). Agriculture, mining, and manufacturing all suffered declines that led to costly short-term borrowing by the government, particularly through International Monetary Fund (IMF) and World Bank (WB) programs. The new government inherited a state with very limited external indebtedness in 1980. However, it joined the IMF in that year and quickly became indebted through IMF borrowing to help cover massive spending on social programs and government expansion in the early 1980s (Kadhani 1986; Stoneman 1988).

These economic difficulties and external political pressures contributed to the call in the July 1983 budget for a one-year halt on the purchase of land for resettlement (Munslow 1985: 53). In 1985 the World Bank warned that a hasty decrease in commercial farmland was potentially devastating for food security (World Bank 1985). Zimbabwe's failure to meet credit targets led to IMF cancellation of the country's stand-by facility (emergency loans available for balance-of-payment problems). The country then went without IMF lending from 1984 to 1987 and hence was fairly resistant to IMF pressure in the mid-1980s. However, since 1980, the World Bank has been Zimbabwe's largest single aid-donor and has thus been able to exert significant leverage over Zimbabwean policy, much of which has been in line with IMF thinking (Kadhani 1986; Stoneman 1988).

There was also an overall shift in development policy by the late 1980s, from one of state-led social and economic transformation to macro-economic policies that encouraged foreign investment, fiscal restraint, and an enhanced role for the private sector. This change is clearly outlined in the *Second Five-Year National Development Plan 1991–1995* (Zimbabwe 1991: "Foreword").

Elsewhere in Africa and the South, WB- and IMF-led structural adjustment packages were well established by this point. In Zimbabwe, it had become clear to the government by the late 1980s that macro-economic policies had to change. Low foreign investment, budget deficits, escalation of debt, increasing inflation, decreasing industrial output, and general infrastructural decay persisted in spite of some good internal economic growth (Lopes 1996). In 1989–90 there was an attempt to formulate a "made in Zimbabwe" adjustment package that took into account government priorities in protecting the significant gains in human development. The 1992 *Human Development Report* of the United Nations Development Program (UNDP) shows that Zimbabwe made gains in the major human development indicators, such as infant mortality, adult literacy, child malnourishment, access to health services, and primary and secondary school enrolment. However, as the IMF/WB stepped in, the traditional package of reforms gradually overtook the made-in-Zimbabwe attempt (Lopes 1996: 18–20). By the early 1990s, economic reform IMF/WB-style was well entrenched with the Economic Structural Adjustment Program (ESAP). This shift meant a stronger focus on private enterprise, such as commercial farming, and less on state-led programs. These moves hurt poorer households, with cuts in health services, skyrocketing inflation, and elimination of important subsidies such as those on basic foodstuffs. As a result, human indicators suffered severe blows, and some of the post-independence gains were virtually wiped out (Lopes 1996; Moyo 1996). Recognizing this trend, the government proposed the Poverty Alleviation Action Plan in 1993, with the support of the UNDP. In so doing, it acknowledged that economic adjustment had not made allowance for equitable treatment and protection of the poor:

Whereas Zimbabwe's economic stabilization and reform programme has assured positive real growth, there is need for effective comparable programmes to ensure equity, and to translate these gains to greater prosperity for the disadvantaged population and poor in general. The levels of social expenditures and per capita growth are still below that required for rapid poverty reduction. At this time, Zimbabwe's social indicators are revealing worrisome decline in social conditions, which coupled with inflation, means severe hardship for the disadvantaged and the poor. (Zimbabwe 1993: 3)

General hardship continued throughout the 1990s, the effects of ESAP having been deepened by a devastating drought in 1992. ESAP did not have the intended economic effects. Inflation continued to soar, while foreign exchange earnings and incomes dropped. High interest rates and high prices for imported goods hampered local businesses and the flow of capital into the country (Lopes 1996; Dashwood 2000; Bond and Manyanya 2002).

The severe fiscal restrictions had definite effects for resettlement, and debates about land reform became increasingly "conservative" (Moyo 1996: 1). While the 1991 plan pledged $400 million to the resettlement program, little of this was ever allocated in succeeding budgets. In 1995 the program was allocated a tiny $10 million, which would cover costs of acquiring only three farms, with nothing left over for infrastructural development. In the 1996 budget, resettlement was given an even smaller allotment of $7 million.[6]

These macro-economic pressures are clearly central. However, there are indications that the new government also gradually adopted a colonial-like ideology, one that separated the problem of environmental degradation in African areas from the issue of equitable access to land and, through this, shifted the discourse from justice to productivity (Vivian 1994; Drinkwater 1989; Elliott 1991; Cliffe 1988a; Wekwete 1991). As noted above, the early post-independence government position placed resettlement at the centre of rural development. While services, agricultural extension, and other developments were to be improved in communal areas, land reform distinctly emphasized "land redistribution." Problems of land deterioration in communal areas were clearly linked to problems of inequitable access to land. By 1985, however, peasant practices in communal areas were increasingly emphasized as part of land reform, while resettlement received less commitment. Volume 1 of the *First Five-Year National Development Plan 1986–91* included a plan to reorganize settlement patterns in communal areas, recognizing that "the programme of land reform and resettlement which were some of the cornerstones of the *Transitional National Development Plan* (TNDP) fell far short of resettling 162 000 families" (Zimbabwe 1986: 28). Volume 2 of the *First Five-Year National Development Plan* named the reorganization of communal areas as a "new feature of the resettlement exercise" (Zimbabwe 1988:

13). In addition, targets for resettlement were significantly reduced. In the 1984/85 budget, the finance minister announced that resettlement efforts would focus on improving infrastructure for existing settlements (Zinyama 1991). This new focus was echoed in the World Bank perspective on resettlement in the 1990s. Christiansen (1993), for example, argues that the pace of resettlement should be slowed to perhaps about 2,000 families per year and that more effort should be put into improving productivity on existing schemes. The 1986–91 plan envisaged settling 15,000 families per year, but these targets went unmet owing to a shortage of land and lack of money to buy what was available (Wekwete 1991).

Influential voices had urged a focus on peasant practices in communal lands and caution regarding the role of resettlement in rural development since independence (Drinkwater 1989). The Riddell Commission of 1981 (Riddell 1981), while noting the need to devote some land to resettlement, recommended "a substantial restructuring and transformation of agricultural production within the peasant sector" (par. 686). The Chavunduka Commission of 1982 recognized the problem of land shortage, but suggested that bad husbandry practices constituted a more serious and fundamental problem:

The main demand for land arises from people with few economic resources who often fail to follow good farming practices. To give these people more land without taking into account the need for major agricultural change will fail to have any long term effect on rural poverty and will result in the depletion of the remainder of Zimbabwe's scarce agricultural resources. Unless this issue is faced squarely there can be no prospect of preserving a healthy and viable agricultural industry. (Chavunduka 1982: par. 266)

The Chavunduka Commission urged caution in focusing on resettlement at the cost of improvement in communal areas: "The Commission is concerned that it may prove financially impossible to run a resettlement programme of this scale and also implement needed development in the neglected communal areas" (Chavunduka 1982: par. 284).

The shift towards accepting these views around the mid-1980s can be attributed in part to "much realignment and realliance of class forces in the country" (Elliott 1991: 85). Although there was still much white control in commercial arenas in Zimbabwe in the 1980s and 1990s, there was some "Africanization" of the bourgeoisie, straining the revolutionary notion that the African state serves the interests of the rural poor majority (Weiner 1988). Like other key areas of the economy, commercial agriculture (and by implication the land allocation issue) entered the "indigenization" discourse. Indigenization simply means the shifting of control of key aspects of the economy from white to black hands, and thus the interests of the rural poor were sidelined in favour of those of large-scale black farmers (Bratton 1994; Nkala 1996).[7] Redistribution of land lacked transparency, and some claimed that it was marked by regional, ethnic, and class biases that favoured elite blacks from the regions and ethnic groups that dominated in the ruling ZanuPF party (Moyo 1996). There were constant whispers of corruption in the 1980s and 1990s, government members being said to have acquired vast parcels of land originally designated for peasant farmers. In the mid-1980s, the government refused to purchase many of the farms on offer, allowing them to go onto the private market. From there, these lands were purchased by wealthy blacks with government connections (Alexander 1994: 337; Munslow 1985: 50–1). The *Guardian Weekly* reported: "In 1992 the Zimbabwean parliament passed the Land Acquisition Act, authorising the government to buy land compulsorily. Two years later it was revealed that the first farms compulsorily purchased had been allocated to cabinet ministers, top civil servants and army generals" (30 June 1996: 4). A call to look into another resettlement scandal was not followed up: "A proper commission of inquiry should be appointed to look into, and establish the veracity of allegations made at the weekend that senior Government officials in Masvingo have taken over a farm earmarked for resettling landless peasants, and that they are helping themselves to the farm. If true, it is a serious case, amounting to a betrayal of the aspirations of hundreds of thousands of Zimbabweans who desperately need land" ("Comment," *Herald*, 1 July 1996: 10).

The issue of corruption in land allocation is central to the current crisis of 2000–4, discussed below. The issue is partly explained by the legacy of racial politics in the country. In the mid-1980s Ibbo Mandaza pointed out that continued white presence served as a convenient excuse for delaying the fulfilment of the population's widespread demands. In other words, the government could blame continued white control for its inability to change the lot of the black majority. At the same time, the white presence served as a justification for government-supported "black empowerment" – the empowering of the rising black middle class and elites. This insight still rang true in the 1990s, perhaps being even more descriptive of the racial rhetoric of politicians. The situation post-2000 is somewhat changed, given the eviction of most of Zimbabwe's white farmers. Somewhat ironically, as discussed below, with the race card now finally played, the corruption of the black elite is stripped bare for all to see.

The stalling on resettlement held throughout the 1990s. Change was slow despite the fact that the government published the National Land Policy in 1991 in preparation for the release from the constraints of the Lancaster House Agreement in 1992, and then passed the Land Acquisition Act, allowing forced selling of land to the government (Masoka 1994). The Land Act removed many of the impediments to land acquisition imposed at Lancaster, and by the mid-1990s between 62,000 and 70,000 families were resettled, but the government estimated that about 200,000 families were waiting for resettlement plots. In 1996 the government began to demarcate commercial farms for resettlement, but the process was stalled by a legal challenge launched by white farmers whose land was demarcated. Nevertheless, in 1995–96 the government claimed to have acquired twenty-three farms, upon which 4,000 people were resettled.[8]

The other major problem consistently named by government in the 1990s, was lack of funds, and government continued to look to Britain, as the former colonial power, for funding assistance.[9]

Clearly, there was a weakening in the government's commitment to the large-scale resettlement of the rural peasantry in the 1990s. This came about partly in response to the reality of international macro-economic forces. It also resulted from the sea change undergone by a liberation force turned government. As the class interest of people in government shifted, the logic of the colonialists that had cast poor peasant farmers as backward and environmentally destructive increasingly made sense. Hence, the 1990s policies of agrarian reform differed little from those of the colonial state. Centralized bureaucratic control and an emphasis on technological change to improve "backward" African practices dominated (Drinkwater 1989; Alexander 1994).

As a result of these shifts in government thinking and practice on resettlement, the terms of the discourse changed. As discussed above, at the beginning, the goals of resettlement were predominantly social and political. However, given the small contribution to commercial agriculture made by the vast numbers of African peasant farmers, the goal of increasing overall commercial agricultural production – by providing viable pieces of arable land, infrastructure, extension services, and access to loan and marketing facilities – was also considered important. In the period 1975–79, for example, the commercial (European) farming sector accounted for about 90 per cent of the value of marketed agricultural produce, Native purchase areas for 2 to 3 per cent, and Tribal Trust Lands (now communal areas) for 5 to 7 per cent (Zinyama 1991). Hence, increasing productivity through resettlement was one of the original goals, but the issue of justice for the landless and the poor came first.

As the government's position on the macro-economic and political pressures (described above) began changing, the emphasis in resettlement increasingly shifted from a goal of justice to one of "productivity." This is reflected in the views of local government representatives in the study site in Wedza District. The resettlement officer stated that the original goals of resettlement had been to uplift the standard of living of the poor and to relieve population pressure in the communal areas. Increasing productivity was a minor issue. The district administrator of Wedza District said much the same thing, holding that the original emphasis was black empowerment. However, by the mid-1990s, there was much more emphasis on productivity.[10] With this shift also came a tendency for government bureaucrats to view small-scale peasant farmers, including those in resettlement, as "inefficient and destructive of land fertility" (Wekwete 1991: 115). Excerpts from the *Herald* express this government view:

Lessons learnt from the past decade and half demand that resettlement programmes be implemented with greater concern shown about their future sustainability. So far, efforts have tended to focus on meeting the immediate needs at the expense of the future.

But such approaches only contribute to creating an environmental wasteland of this country's otherwise rich forests and land ...

The Government wants to formulate a fine-tuned land management programme, which will see resettled villagers receiving knowledge on, and becoming more appreciative of the need to institute better agro-practices and other land use patterns. ("Comment," *Herald*, 20 October 1995)

Farmers told to use land properly: People in resettlement areas must appreciate Government efforts to resettle them by using their land, a senior Agritex officer has said … [He] called for proper land use to maximize on production[,] telling lazy farmers who spent much of their time drinking beer that the land was not meant for burial purposes. (*Herald*, 22 July 1996: 6)

The view that resettlement farmers were lazy and unproductive became conventional wisdom despite the fact that settlers achieved major increases in cash crop production throughout the 1980s. These increases were achieved even while the provision of infrastructure and services had not kept pace with the opening of resettlement schemes and most such schemes were established in marginal agricultural land because of the willing-seller stipulation of Lancaster. The 1980s also saw two debilitating droughts, in 1982/83 and 1987/88 (Bratton 1994; Cliffe 1988b; Wekwete 1991). It is important to note that productivity levels in Model A resettlement schemes varied according to different agro-ecological regions and the prior economic status of the settlers (Bratton 1994: 76–8). However, overall, the Land Tenure Commission of 1994, under Professor Rukuni, found resettlement farmers to be more productive than either communal farmers or small-scale farmers (formerly, those who worked Native African purchase areas): "The conventional wisdom that resettlement areas are unproductive is therefore not objective and contrary to the facts on the ground" (Rukuni 1994, vol. 1: 66).

Clearly, there is a contradiction between government perceptions of resettlement farmers as inefficient and destructive and the farmers' actual achievements. It is argued here that the government's constructing of resettlement farmers in a negative way that obfuscates their real productivity achievements is part of a wider shift away from a commitment to equitable land redistribution. This shift can be traced back to the government's reaction to the dramatic productivity successes of communal area farmers in the first half of the 1980s. Ironically, rather than seeing these achievements as justification for giving more land to small-scale peasant farmers, the government interpreted them as justifying decreased targets for resettlement, as the need to boost small-scale production was seemingly less acute (Moyo 1986; Alexander 1994: 336) – this despite the fact that less than a fifth of the peasantry in communal areas were responsible for the increased productivity. Thus, inequality intensified in rural areas, with many people becoming even more impoverished (Moyo 1986, 1996; Cliffe 1988b; Weiner 1988). All this has meant that increased productivity overall has accompanied increased absolute levels of malnutrition and hunger in communal areas (Jayne et al 1994: 289). These trends, together with annual population growth rates of about 3 per cent since independence, mean that "population pressure and land degradation in the rural areas are more severe today than they were in 1980" (Bratton 1994: 70).[11]

The emphasis on productivity over equitable redistribution was backed up by changes to the criteria for settler selection. In the early days of independence, the landless, returning war refugees, and the poorest people were granted land (Zinyama 1991; Wekwete 1991). In Sengezi, this was indeed the case on the ground, not just on paper. Preferred settlers were refugees or squatters, particularly those whose current status was a result of the war. Special favour was given to those who had been active in the war, either as soldiers or as "helpers" to guerrillas who came to the area, such as *mujibha* (boys) or *chimbwido* (girls) who served the fighters as messagers, cooks, and procurers of clothing and other supplies. People were asked if they had been to Mozambique, Zambia, Botswana, or Tanzania because of the war.[12]

As early as 1982, however, plots were granted to master farmers as well as to the landless poor (Alexander 1994: 333; Munslow 1985: 46). In the mid-1980s, the government perceived that the land was underutilized and that all settlers should have master farmer training (formal training in modern farming techniques by the Agricultural Extension Office) by 1986/87. But as the available land quickly filled up, criteria became even stricter. In the 1990s, applicants had to demonstrate their success as farmers through ownership of such implements as a scotchcart (a wooden, wheeled cart) and a plough. As the minister of lands and water resources, Comrade Kumbirai Kangai, stated, "Land should only be given to people with the potential to fully utilize it."[13] In Wedza District, the district administrator asserted that while there was no shortage of applicants who met the new criteria (there was a waiting list of about 500 people in 1997), allocations were still made to the "needy" – for example, those displaced by developments such as dam construction or the expansion of the growth point (growth points are small commercial centres targeted for development post-1980 where district offices, grain marketing services, and other amenities can be found).[14]

In 1993 President Mugabe appointed a commission of inquiry, headed by Professor Mandivamba Rukuni, to investigate the appropriateness of each land tenure system in the rural areas. These were to be considered "in relation to sustainable resource management, farm productivity and investment" (Rukuni 1994, Executive Summary: iii). The government accepted many of the Land Tenure Commission's recommendations, including those on resettlement.[15] In its analysis of resettlement, the commission stated that tenure insecurity and the weakness of local institutions has meant that common property resources have been poorly managed. It therefore recommended that all current resettlement villages of both Model A family farms, subject to settler agreement, and Model B cooperatives be redemarcated into private holdings that would include homestead, fields, and grazing areas. All new resettlement schemes should follow this pattern. The permit system (discussed in chapter 3) should be abandoned, and settlers given ninety-nine–year leases with options to purchase after an initial ten-year trial period in which they demonstrate serious farming intentions and good practices. This new focus on tenure issues in relation to land reform was consistent with the shift to productivity and efficiency in discourses of land reform.

Along with the focus on land tenure and productive farmers came support for increased productivity of existing settlers and training courses for new ones. Training schemes on model resettlement farms and other special donor projects honed in on a numerically small group of keen and able farmers to boost productivity and launch them as a truly commercial class of farmers.[16] Such efforts were also linked to a concern to reduce the costs to government of resettlement. If the settlers' productivity could be increased, they would become more viable loan risks and hence less dependent on government support. There was also talk of reducing government's burden by making settlers pay for infrastructure.[17]

In the 1980s and 1990s the direction on resettlement was obscured by political grandstanding on the issue of historical land injustice (Moyo 2000). Resettlement became a hot topic in elections and political speeches when revolutionary and anti-white rhetoric was the norm. As one among many examples, President Mugabe was quoted in 1996 as saying in an election speech, "We are now going to use the Land Apportionment Act method they used to take away good land from the blacks. I want to emphasize that we won't buy this land but will acquire it for free" ("Set up land acquisition terms, governors urged," Herald, 7 March 1996). Moyo argues, somewhat ironically in light of the above discussion about the characterizing of resettlement farmers as inefficient, that the anti-white focus of government meant a missed opportunity to argue for land redistribution on the basis of efficiency and productivity. There is ample evidence (as mentioned above) that smaller, peasant-based farming is highly productive if farmers are given the necessary infrastructural and market support. The political rhetoric of the 1990s intensified significantly starting in the year 2000. Raftopolous (2002) argues that the use of the land issue to shore up flagging political support for ZanuPF (particularly in relation to the presidential election of March 2002) in the context of the breakdown of law and order successfully ruptured the link between the land question and the quest for a just, rights-based, post-colonial society. Similarly, Bond and Manyanya point out the irony (and the resultant discursive confusion) in the contrast between official radical anti-imperialism rhetoric and the government's actual practice of following neo-liberal economic policy: "The more the devaluation has hurt prospects for social development, the more that a desperate Robert Mugabe conjured up radical rhetoric to outflank the alienated working class on its Left. Zimbabwean nationalism's 1990s exhaustion had the unintended consequence, perhaps, of reradicalising official discourse" (Bond and Manyanya 2002: 191).

By the mid-1990s, as government faced growing criticism from war veterans' groups and political opponents, government rhetoric often claimed a new urgency regarding the depth and immediacy of the political crisis that loomed as a result of the land shortage for the poor:

The Secretary for Local Government, Rural and Urban Development, Mr Willard Chiwewe, has warned of a second revolution unless Government takes a radical approach in resettling millions of landless Zimbabweans ... Zimbabwe was sitting on a time bomb, which could explode at any time if Government failed to redress land imbalances ... One of the greatest forces for the liberation struggle was for land and at assuming independence, land redistribution was a national need. The landless group is the most volatile. ("Land issue a time bomb: Chiwewe," *Herald*, 29 July 1996)

At the same time, the government warned that there were limits to land redistribution, stating that there was not enough land to satisfy the land needs of the rural poor, even if all commercial land was reallocated. For example, Manicaland provincial governor Kenneth

Manyonda was reported to have addressed the Zimbabwe Farmers' Union in Mutare in the following way:

Zimbabweans should understand that there would never be enough land on which to resettle everyone countrywide, hence land problems would always be there.

Land is inelastic and we cannot have all the land that we want. All we are saying is that there should be equitable distribution of land. Be assured that Government will always encourage commercial farming and see to it that it improves as it is the back bone of our economy. (*Herald*, 15 August 1996: 5)

In the 1990s many members of the most volatile group voted with their feet: they moved onto state, or designated, land and became squatters. The 1982 Chavunduka Report mentioned squatters as already a serious problem, particularly in Victoria Province and the Eastern Districts, commenting that this made planned resettlement difficult, as many of the squatters were ineligible as settlers, either because they were employed or had rights in communal lands (Chavunduka 1982: par. 290–1). In the mid-1990s some observers estimated that over 200,000 families were squatters in communal areas, commercial farms, and state lands (Moyo 1996, 2000). Squatting can be read as the major political response of the rural masses to the pace of official resettlement (Moyo 1996: 24–9). In the 1980s and early 1990s, the government appeared to condone this practice in some areas by following up later with a formal resettlement of squatters.[18] In 1996, however, the minister of lands and water development called for the eviction of 6,000 squatters from state land.[19]

Thus, land occupations have occurred post-independence, with varying intensity, from the early 1980s. While widespread international interest in Zimbabwe's land crisis did not surface until the wave of land occupations in 2000, there was a large wave of occupations in 1998/99. This earlier wave was community led, with "an increasing number of cases of communal farmers invading, *en masse*, large-scale commercial farms" (Marongwe 2002: 22–3). Marongwe describes this earlier wave as follows: "A combination of villagers and farm workers played an important role in the occupations. The major concerns by the villagers were delays by the Government in resettling them and the fact that, in general, they were not informed of the land reform programme. The proximity of the farms to their homes, poor relations between farmers and neighbouring farms and historical land claims by the communities pushed them to occupy farms" (2002: 23). The government reacted negatively to the 1998/99 wave, calling the occupations illegal and resorting to forced evictions in some places: "In enforcing the evictions, there were violent skirmishes when villagers fought running battles with riot police. In extreme situations, villagers were arrested and brought before the courts where they were made to pay fines whilst those who failed to do so faced jail sentences" (Marongwe 2002: 25–6). As they had in earlier occupations in the 1980s and 1990s, villagers targeted state farms, national parks, and state forests as well as large-scale commercial white-owned farms. Like those that came before, the 1998/99 wave expressed people's hunger for land and land entitlement, as well as their critique of government and the race-based inequities of commercial farming. Like those in the mid-1990s, the 1998/99 wave was treated negatively by the government. By contrast, the occupations starting in 2000 were orchestrated by the war veterans and actively encouraged by the government. War veterans mobilized villagers to join the occupations, sometimes using youths to round up villagers, at times coercively (Marongwe 2002: 45). The army and intelligence services also played key roles in providing transport and food to the war vets on the occupied farms (Marongwe 2002: 51). But even this wave of occupations, although supported politically by government, did not remain entirely within government control. For example, in the 2000 wave, some state farms, national parks, and forest reserves were occupied (Marongwe 2002: 27). Many thousands of people were said to have been involved, and an estimated 1,000 to 3,000 white-owned commercial farms were occupied.

It was with the year 2000 wave that the international community, and the Zimbabwean government, recognized that the land issue "time bomb" had indeed exploded. Zimbabwe faced a full-blown political and economic crisis with international ramifications. The large numbers of people involved and the violence against white farmers and among Africans often associated with the occupations attracted the attention of the international press.[20] Zimbabwe experienced high levels of unrest and political uncertainty after its failed constitutional referendum in February 2000 and during the June 2000 general elections. At the end of 2000, the government initiated a fast-track resettlement program that legitimated many of the occupations that had occurred and encouraged many members of the elite, war veterans, and rural folk to begin farming on pieces of formerly white commercial land. International donors, led by the United Nations Development Program and following a 1998 international conference on the land problem in Zimbabwe, had prepared a plan for the gradual redistribution of white commercial land, a plan that included cooperation with white farmers and external funding, especially from Britain.[21] However, this effort was stalled by the Zimbabwean government's continued refusal to compensate white commercial farmers for land gazetted for resettlement. The situation was also complicated by Zimbabwe's participation in the war in the Congo, which caused international donors to hesitate to support the land reform process.[22]

In the years following 2000, violence has increased and further land occupations have occurred. A number of white farmers have been killed, arrested, and imprisoned in this process,[23] and many hundreds of black Zimbabweans, accused of being linked to the opposition party, the Movement for Democratic Change (MDC), have been arrested, tortured, and/or raped.[24] The government claimed that it intended to redistribute 95 per cent of the white commercial land in the country.[25] Throughout 2002 land occupations and evictions continued, and in August of that year 2,900 white farmers were served with eviction notices. Many of the farmers reacted by going to the courts to fight the evictions.[26] In the weeks that followed, according to press reports, 90 per cent of the white farmers in central Zimbabwe were forced to leave their farms, and by October farmers in southern areas were also served with eviction notices and faced arrest if they refused to comply.[27] Reportedly, by early 2004 only 3 per cent of the country's arable land was held by around 400 white farmers, a drastic reduction from the approximately 4,500 farmers who had owned about a third of Zimbabwe's land (but 70 per cent of Zimbabwe's prime farmland) prior to the 2000 occupations.[28] In the meantime and up to the time of writing (April 2004), the international community has been unable to find a way to intervene effectively in a scenario that is seen to jeopardize regional food security, political stability, and international confidence in the region as a whole.

The Commonwealth sent an observer mission to the presidential elections of March 2002, which were widely seen as rigged. Subsequently, a Commonwealth "troika," composed of South African president Thabo Mbeki, Australian prime minister John Howard, and Nigerian president Olusegun Obasanjo, recommended that Zimbabwe be suspended from Commonwealth activities. The suspension was imposed and in March 2003 extended,[29] despite Mbeki and Obasanjo's recommendation that it be lifted.[30] In December 2003 President Mugabe announced Zimbabwe's withdrawal from the Commonwealth.[31] Over the past few years, most foreign governments have pulled out their diplomats and some have banned Zimbabwean politicians from travelling to their countries. Many bilateral agencies and foreign non-governmental organizations (NGOs) have left the country.[32]

In the year 2004, then, the big picture of the land issue is of a volatile race and class struggle in an international arena. The government seems intent on the process of evicting virtually all white commercial farmers. While the government still speaks the rhetoric of redistribution of land to the black peasantry, the elites continue to be the main beneficiaries of land redistribution.[33] Brian Raftopolous (2002) recently stated that the process is really about the takeover of Zimbabwe's main economic asset, agricultural land, by the country's ZanuPF political elite, a sentiment also expressed by the prominent African feminist intellectual Patricia McFadden (2002a). Political theorist David Moore (2001) situates the land grab within an analysis of stalled "primitive accumulation" brought on by colonial and postcolonial structural impediments to economic and political development. Whatever the analysis, the fact is that "the farm invasions have precipitated the widespread erosion or effective collapse of freehold property forms that have underpinned the racialized distribution of land and the consolidation of large-scale capitalist agriculture for over a century" (Worby 2001: 478).

The large questions of race, class, capitalism, and post-coloniality, as outlined in this chapter, paint the broad strokes of the land question in Zimbabwe. How do we fill in the fine brushwork of women and gender between these broad strokes? One of the most important bridges to understanding the gender dimensions in Zimbabwe is the fact that the land reform process is turning out to be ultimately about *exclusion* – not *inclusion* as the ZanuPF government claims – and is accompanied by various discursive strategies, such as anti-white rhetoric or an emphasis on productivity and land tenure, to mask the realities of a closing circle around the "land deserving." Indeed, the trajectory of land reform may reflect little more than a collapsing state's scramble to maintain hegemony by strategically identifying certain groups as among those entitled to land. Whites have clearly become among the excluded. Another of the largest excluded groups, not mentioned thus far, is the commercial farm workers (Rutherford 2001a; Sachikonye 2003):

> The chief victims of the land invasions to receive notice in the international press are white owners and their families who face dispossession with limited compensation, and who have been subjected to various forms of brutality and humiliation, including murder and rape. Yet far greater suffering is borne by their workers who have little in the way of assets but everything in the way of livelihood to lose. As Bill Derman has argued, the so-called fast-track resettlement programme engineered by the farm invasions is "the only land reform in history which will dispossess those who work on the land in far greater numbers than those who will be resettled." (Worby 2001: 491–2)

Women, however, particularly rural peasant women, form another group subject to certain types of exclusion, in their case an exclusion accompanied by gender-specific discursive justification. This book attempts to unravel the nature of this exclusion by examining the roles that gender plays in both state policies and practices and the lived realities of established resettlement farmers. It investigates the gendered nature of resettlement farmers' relationship to the land, taking a case study of one of the original schemes established under the early conditions and spirit of the resettlement program. What opportunities and constraints operated in the original program to influence women's relationship to agricultural land? In pursuit of this question, the book documents an important moment of gendered change in post-revolutionary Zimbabwe and leads us to ask important feminist questions about the current direction of the land reform process.

2 Gendering African Land

"If women want property, then they should not get married."
President Robert Mugabe, August 1994[1]

INTRODUCTION

In this chapter I approach two main tasks. The first is to justify the focus on women and gender in this study through an examination of the power and utility of these social categories in the Zimbabwean context. The second task is to address specifically how women and gender are important in the study of land and land reform, both in Zimbabwe and in the wider context of the region south of the Sahara. In this latter effort, the centrality of the role of the state in relation to gender transformation emerges. This chapter also includes a discussion of the study methodology and an introduction to the study site.

WOMEN AND GENDER

African feminist/womanist scholars have criticized Western feminists for the use of inappropriate concepts or analytical categories.[2] The central feminist concept of gender, however, has been widely accepted by African feminists as a useful theoretical tool. The promotion of scholarship on women as part of a political project of advancing women's interests and improving the material conditions of their lives has also been embraced.[3] However, African scholars have emphasized that "[t]he problematique of gender within Africa ... has to be generated from within the region" (Meena 1992: 1), and have thus called for the development and recognition of distinctly African feminisms (Meena 1992; Nnaemeka 1998).

Clearly, there is a need to problematize the subject "woman" and the concept of gender more vigorously than was the case in the 1970s and 1980s, and to problematize the use of feminist analysis in an African context. Western feminists have responded to this challenge. As attempted most deliberately by Sylvester (1995; 2000), many scholars of women and gender in Zimbabwe have investigated how women are located, defined, differentiated, and shaped by dominant discourses, practices, and ideologies, as well as how they have used their agency to shape their identities and social spaces in colonial and post-colonial times.[4] This book continues this effort to interrogate and make use of the category "woman" in this way.[5]

In the analysis of gender and women in this book, I first question whether the categories "woman" and "gender" relate intelligibly to the social world with which I engage.[6] I have taken my cue from African feminist scholars in the region and from the experiences I had in the seven years that I lived and worked in the region, and have found that this world is undeniably divided into two groups, one called "women" and another called "men," with prescribed roles, rules of conduct, and norms of relations between the two sexes. From an early age, boys and girls undergo intense socialization efforts that produce and code as "natural" gendered divisions of labour, access to economic and cultural resources, identities, roles, hierarchies of privilege, and (compulsory) heterosexual marriage and childbearing (McFadden 1996; Zinanga 1996): "No one questions gender as a meaningful identity and there are men and there are women and everyone knows who is who" (Sylvester 1995: 201). In addition, certain gendered categories have clear rigidities and consistencies that are especially salient to the shape of women's experiences. Marital status and the way that the family mediates access to economic resources, status, and justice emerge over and over again in the work of scholars of gender.[7] This is not to say that "women" as a category is occupied by identical individuals whose experiences can be homogeneously described or assumed to be known. Rather, it is to suggest that there are "modes of power that sustain 'women' as a category, including varieties of marriage, [and] practices that inform administration and policies of 'the state'" (Rutherford 2001b: 150). Furthermore, as Sylvester puts it, "the gender regime" (the discourse of knowledge and power, the practices, laws, customs, social relations, and ideologies that contribute to the differentiation of experience along gendered lines) runs through all "regimes of truth"[8] in both colonial and post-colonial times in ways that disadvantage women:

Viewed benignly, the gender regime "merely" enforces a commonplace designation of two major types of people – men and women. But this designation is rarely benign in its effects on people classified as women. Moreover, the regime of gender, despite many historical permutations and challenges – not the least by "women guerrillas" during Zimbabwe's liberation struggle – continues to be openly advocated in the sense that many people defend "traditional" body-based gender distinctions as a true way of identifying people and designating their social places. (Sylvester 2000: 86)

In other words, there is strong justification for focusing on gender as a central site of struggle for women in rural Zimbabwe. Differences of class, ethnicity, lineage, and totem are also powerful forces shaping women's experiences. A fascinating account of the conflicts that erupted over the installation of a female chief in Matabeleland in the mid-1990s points to how, for example, membership in one social category (first-born child of a chief) can successfully challenge another social category (woman) to disrupt the usual script for women in special cases (Lindgren 2001). However, my own work (especially Goebel 2002a) and that of many others, including that of African feminists as cited above, suggest the centrality of gender designations to women's lives. Rather than being a Western feminist imposition, a focus on gender rapidly emerges as legitimate in fieldwork in Zimbabwe. It is contestation over gender that complicates women's struggle for land rights in Zimbabwe, contestation over which identities, positions, and entitlements women will be able to take up and which not, as read through complex social-cultural meanings, practices, and power. Perhaps the most powerful reason for this, as Kesby has pointed out, is that the relations between land and culture are profoundly about the construction and reconstruction of masculinity (Kesby 1999). This form of masculinity requires women's distance from the land as outsiders in patrilocal settlement, just as it requires women's distance from their children through constructing children as belonging to the patrilineage. Hence, in claiming primary right to land, women create distinctly "regime-defying identities" (Sylvester 2000: 88) for themselves. Historically, culturally, and within current "regimes of truth," for women to claim land in their own right is distinctly to step out place. This book helps to explain why this is so.

WOMEN, GENDER, AND LAND

A great deal has been written about the gendered patterns of African peasant farming in the Southern African region.[9] It has become a truism to state that in societies such as Zimbabwe that are historically hoe cultivating, women are the main farmers but their subordinate cultural and social position often curtails their abilities to farm as productively as possible. Subsistence farming in the region is characteristically insupportable without remittances from husbands working in waged work; hence farming wives remain dependent on husbands' contributions. These contributions may or may not be forthcoming, as husbands frequently become involved in expensive extramarital affairs, drinking, and other town entertainment. African peasant women farmers, therefore, are often pictured in the contradictory position of autonomy by way of *de facto* female headship in the household and of dependency and vulnerability in regard to male earnings and a prevailing gender ideology that condones the supremacy of male authority even in male absence. There are many stories about women who are unable to make key decisions about farming without a husband's authorization and financial support, and about a husband beating his wife because on his return he finds that she has made decisions without his permission or because he feels insecure about his role in the family owing to his unfamiliarity with the rural homestead.

Schmidt (1992a) documents the gendered struggles over production in the African reserves in Rhodesia's colonial history. After initial successes in agricultural production, the viability of African agriculture in the reserves was squeezed through various measures, such as differential pricing and the imposition of various taxes to force male labour migration to serve the needs of European-owned mines and farms. Shona[10] peasant resistance to these measures was strong, but eventually, narrow European interests were served and the reserves were increasingly characterized by *de facto* female-headed households. Although women had been the backbone of peasant agricultural production before colonial interference, male absence left women with an increasingly high farm burden but not necessarily with decision-making authority over farm production. Family dynamics and gender relations changed with colonization. High rates of male migration led to increasing rates of adultery for both husbands and wives, new forms of informal unions, and prostitution. Men's desire to maintain control of their women in the reserves coincided with a colonial interest in keeping women in the reserves to serve as a safety net for retired or redundant workers, as well as to supplement sub-subsistence wages. In the 1920s increasingly harsh patriarchal ideology among African men, supported by chiefs, thus came together with colonial measures (for example, the introduction of passes for women in the 1920s) in an attempt to control women's movements and keep them in the reserves. The "runaway" women flocking to the cities were routinely rounded up and beaten, then returned to their rural homes. Another colonial practice in support of keeping women in reserves was to hire men as domestic workers; this subverted the "natural" association of women with domestic work and served the cause of creating a specifically male waged worked force (Schmidt 1992a, 1992b; Hansen 1992; Jeater 1993; McCulloch 2000).

In the 1930s, to stabilize the workforce, the colonial powers increasingly encouraged men to bring their wives to live with them on commercial farms (Amanor-Wilks 1996). However, a contradictory force operated as the use of female labour increased on commercial farms, since seasonal or casual labour came to be increasingly preferred over a stable, permanent labour force. In practice, however, African men were reluctant to relinquish the security and sense of masculine identity associated with a homestead on a reserve, and their unions with women on commercial farms were often casual or could be characterized as "additional" marriages (Amanor-Wilks 1996).[11] Furthermore, the reluctance of Shona men to work on commercial farms meant that 60 per cent of all farm labour was foreign, mostly Zambian, Malawian, or Mozambiquan, up until 1960 (Weinrich 1979: 18). This statistic fell to 32 per cent by 1975, as whites found that foreigners were more politicized than local Africans (Weinrich 1979: 18). The situation in towns was similar. Rural to urban migration has historically been male dominated (Mandishona 1996). While women have always been among the migrants to town, attempting to flee poverty or patriarchal control in the reserves,[12] the dominant migration pattern has remained one of mobile men who maintain a "real" home in a reserve (now a communal area), presided over by a wife or wives.

In the mid-1990s it was estimated that about 70 per cent of rural households in Zimbabwe were *de facto* female headed (Mandishona 1996). In this context, women play the role of primary farm worker and household manager, with the husband (ideally) providing inputs (seed, equipment, fertilizer, etc.) through earnings from wage work. In most cases, a woman's entitlement to the land and home in a communal area comes through her marriage to a man who has rights to a plot in that particular area, although widows and divorced women may get access to small plots in their natal or married areas. Hence, while rural women's lives have been distinctly tied to the land, this relationship to land has historically been mediated through male entitlement and control through the institution of marriage and the allocative powers of mostly male traditional authorities. Despite irregularities associated with communal tenure, as discussed in chapter 1, the gendered aspect of land allocation appears remarkably consistent, being one of those rigidities, one of those "modes of power that sustain 'women' as a category" (Rutherford 2001b: 150). At the general level, this is a common story throughout the region south of the Sahara (Gray and Kevane 1999).

In the Zimbabwean context, women's lack of primary land rights was historically underpinned by the definition of their legal status as minors and the dual legal system that placed most African women under the dictates of customary law in the colonial period (Stewart et al 1990; Maboreke 1991). After independence, in 1982, the new government instituted the Legal Age of Majority Act (LAMA), which gave women majority status at age eighteen. Despite the provisions of LAMA, customary law still dominated legal practice in communal areas throughout the 1980s (Maboreke 1991; Stewart 1992). This meant that women did not gain access to communal area land in their own right, but the practice of assigning land mainly to married men continued (Chimedza 1988). Further, in customary law, a widow does not inherit entitlement to the land upon the death of a husband, but keeps it in trust for the male heir, usually the eldest son. She may even be chased away by the relatives of the deceased.[13] In the contemporary context, one of the central calls of the national feminist movement is the formal entitlement of women to land.[14]

There is an emerging consensus in the feminist literature on women and land in Africa south of the Sahara that securing land rights for women is central to improving both women's livelihoods and food security more generally (Razavi 2002: 16). There are debates about the type of land tenure that would best achieve these goals, especially a questioning of the potential impacts of introducing privatized individual tenure (favoured by the World Bank) in contexts where some forms of communal multi-use and multi-user systems may in fact protect some land access for women and other marginalized groups (Whitehead and Tsikata 2001 cited in Razavi 2002). MacKenzie, for example, found that in Kenya privatized tenure under a titling system can erode women's land rights (MacKenzie 1990). This issue is discussed further in chapter 5. In other contexts, such as Uganda, it has been shown that it is not lack of access to land but a shortage of inputs, including capital and labour, that limits women's farming productivity (Razavi 2002). In the Zimbabwean context, in the current legal framework wherein customary laws of inheritance are most likely to be applied, individualized tenure may indeed marginalize women. However, the evidence presented in this book makes it clear that women's land entitlements are overly vulnerable to the whims of male largess, whether the largess of state agents, local chiefs and headmen, husbands or husbands' relatives. Strengthening the security of women's tenure is unquestionably an important goal.

As discussed at length in subsequent chapters, Zimbabwe's early resettlement program of the 1980s and 1990s made a limited response to this concern, facilitating some improvements in land rights for some women. However, these moves always remained circumscribed within particular definitions of gender relations within marriage.

Women's chances of achieving the goal of primary land rights seem even more remote in the early twenty-first century than they did in the 1980s and 1990s. In 1998 and 1999, in a series of cases, most notably *Magaya vs Magaya*, the Zimbabwe Supreme Court successfully challenged women's legal equality as supported by LAMA (Stewart et al 2000: 23). In the *Magaya vs Magaya* inheritance case, the five judges unanimously agreed that a woman had no rights to her deceased father's estate, ruling that it is "the nature of African society that women are not equal to men. Women should never be considered adults within the family, but only as a junior male or teenager."[15] A coalition of women's groups attempted to influence the constitutional reform process in 1999 and get women's equality rights written into the constitution. However, the process culminated in the public rejection of the government's proposed constitution in February

2000.[16] Currently, Zimbabwe's constitution does not protect women's equality rights, allowing them to be overruled by customary law.

Indeed, after the Zimbabwean state's initially somewhat positive (if contradictory) engagement in the 1980s with issues of gender equality (e.g., it set up the Ministry of Community Development and Women's Affairs, subsequently inacted LAMA, and made some important special provisions for women in the resettlement process), gender issues have been increasingly marginalized and transformed in state discourse. Gender equality as a project of the state has moved from a (mostly) positive issue to an issue that at times is cast as a challenge to the project of Zimbabwean nationalism (Ranchod-Nilsson 2001). Some scholars view this situation as part and parcel of the inherited patriarchal dynamics of the state, which in its very nature requires an "othered," non-political, subservient female identity for women in Zimbabwe (Jirira 1995). Others have pointed out various specific practices and characteristics that reflect the state's patriarchal nature. Cheater and Gaidzanwa, for example, discuss the state's attempts to control the burgeoning cross-border trading that thousands of Zimbabwean women took up in the 1990s in response to the economic hardships brought on by the Economic Structural Adjustment Program (ESAP). Both the cross-border mobility and the economic independence of the activity, they argue, offended the sense of gender propriety of the elite males of the state (Cheater and Gaidzanwa 1996). As noted above, in colonial times, as a result both of custom and of colonial state policy, women's mobility was curtailed, and according to Cheater and Gaidzanwa, the endurance of this legacy is seen in the treatment of female cross-border traders.

Another telling example of the patriarchal nature of the post-colonial state is in citizenship policy as expressed in the 1984 Citizenship Act. Zimbabwean men who marry foreign women can transfer their citizenship to their wives, but women who marry foreign men cannot transfer such rights to their husbands or children and also face the diminishment of their own citizenship rights (McFadden 2002b). This notion of citizenship reflects patrilineal patterns common in Shona culture, wherein a man stays within his patrilineal family upon marriage, while a woman acquires obligations to her husband's family upon marriage. She often moves to the husband's area but still maintains obligations and rights within her natal home. Hence, the citizenship policy not only violates women's equality rights, but also

imposes an androcentric view of culture, as women's bilineal experience of rights and obligations is violated through a policy that recognizes uni-allegiance only along patrilineal lines. As Cheater and
Gaidzanwa note, this deployment of neo-traditionalism for patriarchal purposes contains elements of exclusion – that is, a narrowing
of eligibility for key rights such as citizenship and mobility at a time
when women are increasingly mobile across international borders
and increasingly likely to marry foreign men. The boundaries around
the category "woman" are therefore shrinking, delimiting the activities and identities deemed legitimate for women's full membership
in society. Further, these practices are explained and justified through
the imposition of culture as read from the position of black male elites.

We also see these exclusionary practices in relation to the selection
of "legitimate" recipients of resettlement land. State representatives
frequently explain not extending primary or even joint land rights to
married woman as a reluctance to "interfere with culture": "In a
response in August 1994 to the suggestion by a rural woman that
land permits in resettlement areas be registered jointly in the names
of spouses, President Mugabe of Zimbabwe asserted that 'if women
want property, then they should not get married'"(Cheater and
Gaidzanwa 1996: 200). The language used here is interesting in that
it explicitly demonstrates that equal rights for women are considered
to contradict women's main cultural and social identity (as married
women). The state's response to women's call for equal rights to land
is thus to threaten them with social exclusion. This issue is discussed
further in subsequent chapters. Here it is important to connect these
exclusionary patterns with other patterns of exclusion in relation to
land reform. As discussed in chapter 1, the land reform process has
been characterized by increasingly exclusionary definitions of legitimate recipients of resettlement land. Clearly, married women in their
own right are off the list.

State hostility towards women has meant that women's feminist
activism in Zimbabwe has been predominantly and increasingly
located outside of the state in civil society and that international
feminist networks and support have become crucial to the vibrancy
of the struggle for gender justice (Cawthorne 1999; Davison 1997;
Geisler 1995; McFadden 2002c). Indeed, disillusionment with the
state, along with the cruel progress of HIV/AIDS and the ravages of
high unemployment, has fostered more radical and post-structuralist
elements in the women's movement and feminist academe in the

country.[17] However, while the power of the state is incomplete (this is demonstrated below in the discussion of women's experiences of the law at the grassroots), it is nevertheless formidable and victories for the women's movement have been slow to materialize. Certainly, the gender identity of "women as equal to men" in a rights-based framework has not been successfully produced.

In this overall rather grim historical and contemporary context for women, and given the current crisis in the land reform process more generally, the possibility for state commitment to gender justice in Zimbabwe's post-Independence land reform process appears dim. Will the land reform process reinforce women's inequitable relationship to land or will it provide new opportunities to improve their position? Are there opportunities for women to gain primary access to land? As the evidence presented in this book documents, important gains were made for women in the first stage of resettlement, despite overarching structural problems, ongoing cultural resistance deployed by local patrilineal practices, and an increasingly hostile state. Will these gains be lost as the new dynamics of the land process emerge? And finally, if feminist activists can successfully push for positive state support utilizing a rights-based framework, how can such a framework be evaluated within the deepening deployment by the state of neo-traditional culture and values?

THE ROLE OF THE STATE

The support of the state was crucial in the opening up of certain spaces for women in the early resettlement process. The notion of the key role of state support for social justice remains current in the literature on gender and agriculture in Africa. In a recent book documenting the pressures of neo-liberalism on gender and agriculture in Africa, the editor writes: "The state has a clear mandate from its citizens for the provisioning of a decent standard of living and an overall sense of social justice – the state needs to be pressured, monitored, and reformed in order to fulfil this mandate, but not bypassed" (Razavi 2002: 33).

However, it is important to pursue further the question of the role of the state, especially through law and policy, as an agent for gender justice for women. Zimbabwean feminists have been critiqued for relying too much on the state's support of change (Moyo 1995), a reliance that arguably reifies the state as a rational engine of social reform. The discussion thus far has suggested that the state is far from rational. Worby has pointed out the following tendencies in relation to discourse on land reform:

One of its central elements is a set of persistent assumptions about the *state*: first, that it already is, and must be in future, the arbiter of all significant agrarian conflict, whether overt or latent; second, that it must also be the principal agent of any reallocation of rights in property; and third, that "it" is both obligated and destined to make such reallocations in accordance with a land-use plan that is both *rational* and national, in which every tenure and population category has its just quantum of moral space and its appropriate territorial place. (Worby 2001: 489)

Drawing on Moyo, Worby suggests that the state is much more heterogeneous than often assumed and that it is involved in complex negotiations with rural people and institutions that shape state policies and practices. In other words, the state must be understood as enmeshed in, rather than distinct from, society. What are the implications for understanding the impact of state land policy on women and gender relations?

The work of Women and Law in Southern Africa Research Trust (WLSA) on women and the state in Zimbabwe is helpful here. Throughout the post-independence period, WLSA has studied the legal situation of women. Its primary focus has been the documentation of women's often-contradictory legal status under the two systems of customary and general law and their generally poor access to and knowledge of their legal rights (Armstrong and Ncube 1987; Stewart et al. 1990; Maboreke 1991; Stewart 1992; Ncube and Stewart et al. 1997; Stewart et al. 2000). WLSA has also produced findings that show "that women are marginalized from direct access to and control of resources such as material resources, including land and enabling resources such as education and skills training" (Stewart et al. 2000: 13). Additionally, and more important here, WLSA has produced nuanced studies of the dynamic and interconnected nature of the dual legal system, explaining how it actually plays out in people's lives and making it clear that the customary and general systems are not rigidly bifurcated: "people move freely between customary law and general law picking and choosing their remedies as they meet their needs" (Stewart et al. 2000: 13). WLSA research has also pointed out that the actual delivery of justice operates through both formal and informal institutions. The former includes chiefs' courts and the state court system, and the latter includes family councils, churches, Village Development Committees, and civil society bodies. Furthermore, in local contexts, institutions frequently outstrip the formal parameters of their legal mandates: "Adjudication processes tend to respond to the needs that are evident in the community. For example it is common knowledge that chiefs and headmen exercise jurisdiction way beyond their formal legal mandates. Also local bodies such as the Village Development Committees (VIDCOS) adjudicate on local disputes, even though they do not have formal authority to do so" (Stewart et al. 2000: 19–20). Women's access to legal justice is affected by this "plurality of decision making fora" as well as by "the hegemony of the family over many women's lives ... [and hence] many of the problems women face are regarded as social and family-based problems and are seen as requiring family-based solutions. Consequently many aspects of women's lives are dealt with in the private realm of family and local community rather than in the public domain of the formal law" (Stewart et al. 2000: 13).

These findings have led WLSA to the following conclusion: "The power and reglementary [sic] capacity of families, religious bodies, community groups and traditional authorities over women's actions had been clearly revealed by previous WLSA studies. Thus it became necessary to problematize the scope and effect of these bodies in relation to the more common understanding of justice delivery that is implying the intervention of the state" (Stewart et al. 2000: 16). Altogether, WLSA's research calls us to attend to how customary and general law, as well as traditional and cultural practices, all jostle together in the everyday lives of women. This leads us to ask the following crucial question: "One question that such an approach postulates is whether justice is, ought to be or in reality can be, the prerogative of the state and its authorized agencies or is something that can be found and delivered in a multiplicity of ways and at many sites, including those not recognized by the state?" (Stewart et al. 2000: 20).

The implication for women and land rights is that while state intervention is crucial to the improvement of women's access and control of land, at the end of the day, women will have to negotiate those rights through the complex social field of formal and informal institutions (especially families) and through customary and general law practices and values. WLSA captures this process in its concept of women operating "in the shadow of the law": "[Women] are located in semi-autonomous social fields that create their own norms for regulating behaviour but are not divorced from the formal law – thus their semi-autonomous nature" (Stewart et al. 2000: 24).

This explanation of rural women vis-à-vis institutions, practices, and ideas about law and justice delivery is paralleled strongly by the experiences of women who have engaged with the state through resettlement policy. While women made important gains partly through provisions of the state, advances came with a struggle on the ground and within the parameters laid out by a patriarchal state as well as patriarchal local institutions, practices, and ideologies. Early resettlement policy and practices also left most women deeply vulnerable in terms of their land rights and security.

In the remainder of this chapter, I introduce the study proper, first describing the study methodology and then the study site.

METHODOLOGY

Fieldwork

The main fieldwork for this qualitative study took place between 1995 and 1998. During this time I was affiliated with the Institute for Environmental Studies at the University of Zimbabwe, and until 1997 I was a PhD student in the Department of Sociology at the University of Alberta. Most of my research was carried out in the Sengezi Resettlement Area, Wedza District, Zimbabwe. In Sengezi I employed multiple methods, including participatory rural appraisal (PRA), formal interviews with villagers from four villages in Sengezi, field assistant diaries, personal observation, and informal interactions with local people during my approximately twenty visits to the area. I also carried out several key informant interviews with local officials and leaders and conducted documentary, archival, and newspaper research and analysis.

Early on in the research process, I was fortunate to make good friends with Nyaradzo Dzobo (Mrs Shayanewako) and her husband, Charles Shayanewako. Mr Shayanewako is a teacher at the local secondary school in the study site, and he and his wife kindly took me into their home for the duration of my many field visits.

In order to minimize my own preconception of the issues and problems, I adopted a gradual approach to the study. There were no pre-planned interview schedules or questionnaires, and the information gathered at one stage led to the design of a research plan for a later stage. I began with *initial visits*, in which I talked to village chairmen, the resettlement officer, the ward councillor, and the district administrator, seeking their permission to do the study. When permission was granted and the interest and enthusiasm for the study was clear, I proceeded to the next phase: *general village meetings*. In these meetings I introduced myself and described the project in general terms. General questions and answers followed, as well as a discussion of what people perceived as their land and resource problems. I also asked people about the local history. Then we set dates for the next research phase, *participatory rural appraisal*. After the general meetings, a few key villagers accompanied me on drives around the village resource areas, and we took the opportunity to discuss resource issues, boundary disputes, and so on.

When I arrived in Zimbabwe, there was considerable interest in participatory rural appraisal methods in natural resource studies, partly as a result of Louise Fortmann's influence during a stint at the Centre for Applied Social Sciences (CASS) at the University of Zimbabwe (Fortmann 1996). I attended a training workshop on PRA methods held at Gwaai in August 1995, hosted by the International Development Research Centre and the Canadian International Development Agency in cooperation with the Institute of Environmental Studies at the University of Zimbabwe. From what I learned, PRA methods seemed a good entry point for a rural study on land and natural resources. Also, because PRA was a major emergent methodology in developmentalism, I wished to test it as part of my overall investigation of developmentalism. I designed a two-day PRA workshop for my study villages, and with the help of an expert PRA trainer, Nontokozo Nemarundwe (née Nabane) from CASS, I trained four research assistants from my study villages in PRA methods.

PRA methods have many positive aspects (Goebel 1998; Fortmann 1996). The most transparent of these is that it allows the researcher to gather, in an efficient manner, a large amount of preliminary data that could otherwise take much time and effort. Another positive aspect is related to local power dynamics. Scholars of development are increasingly aware that attention to indigenous knowledge is not enough. Knowledge is embedded in power relations. There is thus no single indigenous or local knowledge; rather there are competing perspectives. Some dominate, while others are marginalized (Scoones and Thompson 1994; Mosse 1994). PRA can provide an opportunity to observe some power relations in action, but it can also work to hide local power relations. Emphasis on group work, on consensus in data expression and presentation, is particularly prone to the silencing of marginal or dissident views. I divided villagers into men's and women's groups, knowing that this might mean getting the views primarily of the dominant women and men among them.

As a public event, PRA can stumble when the topic is sensitive. My research at times ventured into illegal activities in resource use, such as cutting live trees, selling natural resource products like firewood, hunting game, and netting fish. Hence, I expected that information on rules and their breaking might be distorted in the public PRA process. Getting a clear picture of people's practices involved much more than asking them, in a public setting, to describe them.

Discovering that PRA data are not clear-cut is neither a surprise nor a disaster for social researchers, particularly when they embrace qualitative methodologies. Accounts are always representations or social constructions. However, they are also accounts of something (Moore and Vaughan 1994). Like Moore and Vaughan, I am willing to accept accounts as both social constructions and data. However, while interrogating people and contextualizing contradictions and complexities, I try to draw out some coherent themes and stories from the PRA data, as well as the data gathered in later work. Some types of data can be treated as more factual than others. I have, for example, accepted people's descriptions of gendered divisions of labour as true to the prevailing ideology but not necessarily true to practice. Because I used an interrogative approach to the PRA data, I believe it has yielded valid clues and starting points of inquiry into the social world of the study area.

After completing the PRA workshops and analysing the massive amounts of data (mostly on large pieces of messy chart paper), I constructed a number of interview question sets for individual household interviews, group interviews, and key informant interviews. Colleagues at the University of Zimbabwe (especially Alois Mandondo, Billy Mukarmui, and Bruce Campbell) provided feedback on my interview schedules, and Mr Mandondo translated the questions into Shona. I have relied much more heavily on the data gathered through these interviews than on the PRA data. Most of the interview schedules use open-ended questions to encourage detailed answers and reduce the controlling aspect of set questions. The formal interviews with villagers are central, as they provide local people's perspectives, which are of primary interest in this study. In different rounds of interviews, we interviewed different samples of villagers from the four Sengezi villages in the study. The samples were chosen on the basis of wealth-ranking information generated in the PRA exercises so that the stratified samples would reflect the different wealth groups in the villages. In this phase, three hundred individual interviews were conducted in five rounds of interviews. Group interviews with nine gender-segregated groups on the subject of divisions of labour (N = 70) were also carried out in this phase.

Next, my head research assistant, Nyaradzo Dzobo, conducted fifty interviews with widows, divorcees, and people who knew the details of the stories of women who had left the area after a divorce, which was most often the case. These interviews were all with women from the Sengezi Resettlement. Ms Dzobo also interviewed fifteen traditional healers (some from Sengezi and some from nearby Buhera Communal Area) and fifteen villagers on the topic of husband-taming herbs. We identified individuals with the relevant experiences through our village networks. All interview transcripts were translated by Mrs or Mr Shayanewako.

Throughout this book I give authority to key informant views where these represent specialized knowledge or concur with the views held more broadly by villagers. Key informants include the resettlement officer, the Agricultural Extension (Agritex) worker, district-level Forestry Commission and Natural Resources Board staff, the district administrator for Wedza, local clinic staff, the local secondary school headmaster, the village chairmen from the four study villages in Sengezi, the ward councillor, and the local ZanuPF chairman.

I also draw on data gathered during my work as PRA coordinator for the Social Forestry Program in 1997–98 in Wedza District, a project undertaken by the German Development Cooperation (GTZ) in cooperation with the Forestry Commission. These data include documentary research from the Wedza District Council and PRA data from ten villages in Wedza District, including four resettlement villages in Sengezi (Goebel and Nabane 1998). Finally, on a brief field trip to Zimbabwe in June 2002, I was able to access government and NGO documents produced since 1998 and talk to people and groups active around the land issue, such as scholars at the University of Zimbabwe, the Women and Land Lobby Group, and ZERO-Regional Environment Organization.

Other Sources

For local history, I have relied on oral historical accounts by key informants and on published secondary sources. For perspectives on colonial and post-colonial policies and perceptions, I have relied on published secondary sources and government documents. In the case of published sources, I have in many cases tracked down the original documents and slightly altered interpretations in the historiography.

For resettlement, environmental, political, and economic issues, I have consulted the government-controlled local press – the *Herald* and the *Sunday Mail*, and the local independent press – the *Zimbabwe Independent*, *Speak Out*, *Moto*, *Sapem*, the *Financial Gazette*, and *Women Plus*. I have also consulted many unpublished, or "working paper," documents from various departments of the University of Zimbabwe. These latter are particularly important, as they represent work of local scholars who face various obstacles in publishing their work in refereed international journals and hence can be effectively invisible to the foreign researcher. Since being out of Zimbabwe, I have accessed ZWNEWS, a daily online compilation of media stories on Zimbabwe from around the globe.

Positionality, Identity, and Research in Africa

African feminist/womanist theorists, like other non-Western or Third World feminist scholars (e.g., Mohanty 1991; Ong 1988), offer important critiques of Western feminist scholarship. I have already discussed how they have challenged Western theoretical categories and concepts. Another aspect of their work that relates to this book involves the race and class politics of knowledge production. African theorists have critiqued "the western monopoly over the production of knowledge" (Meena 1992: 3),[18] including knowledge produced about Africa. Foreign scholars, they argue, often ignore the work of African-based scholars and fail to appreciate how race and class privilege enables their own work while working against the funding and publishing of African-based scholars. Foreign scholars, according to the African theorists, have rarely questioned their own cultural biases with much vigour, and the dominant scholarly result has been a perception of African women as the ultimate victims of patriarchal and colonial oppression. This discursive move obscures African women's lived realities (Nnaemeka 1997; Lewis 2000). Western feminists have, for example, consistently misinterpreted African women's experiences of motherhood and other "female sphere" work and values, and failed to identify women's agency (Ibrahim 1997; Nfah-Abbenyi 1997).

For many Western feminist scholars, these types of critiques have "created a major identity crisis" (Wolf 1996: 1). As Diane Wolf points out, the dilemmas that have arisen for Western feminists who have undertaken cross-cultural research, particularly field-based research, "gnaw at our core, challenging our integrity, our work, and at times, the raison d'etre of our projects" (Wolf 1996: 1). While I most decidedly do not want this book to be about me and my encounters with the people of the Sengezi Resettlement, there are ethical and epistemological questions that must be raised with the type of project I have undertaken. In my research I have self-consciously situated myself in the research process as a person of racial and economic privilege in comparison to the people of the Sengezi Resettlement. By virtue of my white skin, I automatically participate in racially based power relations. Despite the liberation of Zimbabwe from white rule in 1980, white Zimbabweans continue to be privileged economically and the values and institutions of Western society, such as formal education and capitalist development, remain central to local people's aspirations. Success and advancement continue to be racially marked categories in Zimbabwe, and hence my whiteness automatically elevated me in people's eyes, as did the evidence of my long years of formal education. As a Canadian, I was also draped with privilege in the eyes of many local people, as Canadians were perceived (rightly or wrongly!) as generous with regard to development aid and as politically supportive during the war of liberation. This positive view of me by local people was further enhanced by their knowledge that I had been a secondary school teacher in Chiweshe District in Zimbabwe in the 1980s, an obvious sign to them of my interest and commitment to Zimbabwe's development. As a wife and mother of three children, I was also an acceptably attached, heterosexual female, a positionality that was very important in helping me establish communication with women in the area and protecting me from (some) advances from local men. The privileged position these many attributes bestowed upon me no doubt partially explains the respect, generosity, and cordiality with which I was received in Sengezi.

However, as Daphne Patai has so rightly pointed out, a self-reflexive acknowledgment of privilege does nothing to change the inequalities upon which that privilege is based (Patai 1994; Wolf 1996: 35). Elsewhere, Patai has insisted that for this reason it is not possible for Western feminists to do ethical research involving Third World women (Patai 1991). While conscious of the ethical dilemmas, I remain unconvinced that the appropriate response is withdrawal, particularly when I have been encouraged by numerous African scholars in Zimbabwe to continue my work. While no research process is yet available that might mitigate existent social inequalities, there is still a profound need to document and engage with these inequalities in scholarship and politics. After all, the engines and institutions of development, including "women and development" projects and policies, most of which do not problematize the role of the Western outsider in Third World contexts, will continue with or without self-reflexive feminist academics (Wolf 1996: 35). Academics thus have a role in promoting analyses and processes in Western-based institutions working in Africa that challenge the embedded hierarchies of race, class, and gender. In addition, and more importantly to me personally, attention to the dilemmas of cross-cultural research and the power relations of knowledge production can lead to collaborative research with local academics, resulting in both better-informed research and the erosion of Western dominance in the world of knowledge production. In my own case, my many informal discussions, seminars, and workshops with local scholars at the University of Zimbabwe and my field research collaboration with Nontokozo Nabane helped me see where my understandings were distorted and educated me about the categories and research problems that local scholars saw as important.

Nevertheless, given the cultural, racial, economic, and linguistic distance between myself and the participants in my study, there were limits on the extent to which I could interpret the information gathered. Using a qualitative approach to the field research, I have attempted to identify and employ local people's perceptions and analyses (see above). I have also checked many aspects of my analysis with some of the local people I worked with, through village report-back sessions, as well as with local Zimbabwean scholars. Ultimately, however, this account remains that of an outsider and academic who has tried, but may nevertheless have failed, to adequately interrogate her own biases and perceptions: "Every anthropologist and historian knows that one comes to understand the politics, agriculture, and ecology of an area through practical engagement which both grounds and goes beyond intellectual appreciation, but knowing this does not always allow us to see exactly where our knowledge comes from and what it inheres in" (Moore and Vaughan 1994: xxi).

THE STUDY SITE:
THE SENGEZI RESETTLEMENT AREA

The following description is based on conditions in the late 1990s. Today, in 2004, as a result of the land occupations, the rich tobacco farms are no longer in operation. I use the ethnographic present here and throughout the book when referring to field-based material.

The Sengezi Resettlement Area, near Wedza growth point, is about 170 kilometres southeast of Harare, along the Seke Road. The trip from Harare takes you through Seke and Chiota Communal Areas and then into rich tobacco-growing commercial farms. The contrast between these two types of land areas, especially when the tobacco crop is in full leaf, is striking and heartbreaking, speaking as it does to the land crisis for African farmers. Next to the rich tobacco lands lies the Sengezi Resettlement Area.

Established in 1981, Sengezi lies in natural regions II and III, with mean annual rainfall at about 800 mm/yr (Kinsey 1986). Zimbabwe is classified into five natural agro-ecological regions for the purpose of commercial farming, based mainly on average annual rainfall. The regions are decreasingly viable from regions I down to V. Regions IV and V receive little rainfall and are considered suitable only for extensive livestock and game ranching. Region III is suitable for semi-intensive farming based on both livestock and crop production. Regions I and II are the only regions with reliable rainfall and suitable for intensive crop and livestock production. As most land acquired for resettlement in the 1980s was on a willing-seller basis, the program tended to acquire land in regions III, IV, and V rather than in the better regions II and I (Zinyama 1991). Sengezi's region III designation indicates that the area is quite well suited to semi-intensive crop and livestock production. The Sengezi scheme is bordered by two communal areas, Save North and Wedza, and also shares a border with actively farmed commercial land. The area is still well wooded, especially in comparison to the communal areas that border it, although settlers say it is extensively deforested compared to when they arrived in 1981. The commercial farms that formerly made up the resettlement area were used either as tobacco or cattle-ranching farms. These farms were abandoned by their white owners during the war of liberation in the late 1970s. Soil types are variable, even within short distances. Some settlers have very good fields, while others struggle with sandy soils or heavy soils that drain poorly. The landscape is dominated by Wedza Mountain, which lies to the south in Wedza Communal Area. It is a sacred mountain, and the Rhodesian Army used it as a base during the guerrilla war in the 1970s. The resettlement scheme proper is dotted with small rocky hills, which tend to be well wooded, and rows of tall eucalyptus planted by the former white farmers.

Ethnically, most of the people in this area are part of the Shona.[19] In the Wedza area, the original, autochthonous spirits are of the Rozvi dynasty, which ruled from the late seventeenth century up to 1840, when it was defeated by the Ndebele (Beach 1980; Bourdillon 1987). Although there are still members of the Rozvi totem in the area, they no longer dominate. Local history states that the Rozvi gave the leadership to the Jena clan because the Jena were good fighters and would look after the area. It is said that the Jena were so named because one of them married an old white-haired woman of the Rozvi clan ("Jena" means "white"). The Rozvi were so grateful that they bestowed leadership of the Wedza area on this new dynasty, "the Jena." The current chief is of the Jena totem. The Jena have established many sacred areas for their ancestral spirits, such as in Wedza Mountain.[20]

In the resettlement area, although families are in frequent touch with their own family ancestors, there is little awareness of the autochthonous spirit guardians. When asked about what happened to the original spirits, almost half of the inhabitants (42 per cent) say they do not know. About a third of the people say that these spirits left, having been chased away when the whites occupied the land. A smaller number of people say that the spirits left because the settlers are not appeasing them. About 12 per cent of the sample say that the original spirits are indeed there. Among these, most feel that these spirits are unhappy, some adding that this is clear from the frequent droughts. The interconnections of spirit guardians, ancestors, land, and drought are discussed further in chapter 6.

Within the Sengezi Resettlement Area I chose four of the original six villages established in 1981. By 1996 there were seventeen villages in the scheme. In general, each of the original villages occupies the area of a former commercial farm. Typically, the large old farmhouse lies in ruins, a reminder of the bloody war and an enduring testament to the architectural dimensions of black/white rural inequality. Settlers are grouped as family units in nucleated villages, close to the access roads. Each household has a "stand," a plot of about half an acre, upon which sits one rectangular, cement, asbestos-roofed house, generally used both as a bedroom for the parents and as a formal sitting room. There is also a smaller cement structure that contains a pit toilet. Both of these structures were built by the resettlement authority, with the cost recorded as a debt owed by each settler. According to the resettlement officer, most people have not paid this debt, which had quadrupled in value by 1996. The homesteads also have a (usually round) kitchen hut, built of the more traditional materials of mud bricks, poles, and thatched roofs. These kitchens, which are of the traditional Shona type, have a fire pit in the centre at which most of the family's meals are prepared, with firewood the fuel. Kitchen utensils are stored here, and meals are usually eaten inside. Other structures on the plot include a granary of mud, poles, and thatch, a high wooden structure where the harvested grain is dried, and perhaps another structure for keeping chickens. If grown married children still live with the family, a second kitchen hut or bedroom may be built. Generally, families plough a small home field at the homestead, where they grow maize, pumpkins, or even potatoes. In Village 1, which has piped water at each homestead, people generally keep a market garden in their home field. In other villages, women establish gardens in wetland areas.

Each household is allocated five hectares (twelve acres) of arable land, which, in a good year, is capable of yielding at least ten tonnes of maize. An average family needs about two tonnes for consumption, so this leaves a healthy remainder as a cash crop. Countrywide, nearly 90 per cent of households in communal areas each have a total landholding of only ten acres or less. Only part of this would be arable (Rukuni 1994, 3:463). Indeed, about 58 per cent of communal area farmers have arable landholdings of less than two and a half hectares (Rukuni 1994, 3:108). Thus, the allotment of five hectares of arable land in resettlement areas implies a significant increase of arable land for most small-scale farmers.

Farmers in Sengezi plant most of their area with maize, but they also plant other subsistence and cash crops such as sunflower, rapoko (finger millet), groundnuts (peanuts), beans, and in a few cases sorghum, rice, and soybeans. The Agritex worker wanted to establish tobacco, but farmers are reluctant to take the risk and find it difficult to cooperate over the construction of a shared tobacco barn. Only seven farmers had tried tobacco by 1997. The rainy season usually begins in November, when people plough and plant their rain-fed fields. From November through February, people are very busy weeding and cultivating in the fields. Harvesting takes place from March through June. The dry winter months of July and August are restful months of much visiting and eating (and hence a good time for fieldwork!).

Each household has the right to put to pasture seven livestock units in the common property grazing lands allocated to each village. In actuality, some households have many cattle and others none or few. Households "borrow" grazing land from those who are not using it. This is also true of fields, with some successful farmers nearly doubling their hectarage through borrowing. Altogether, the mean area available per household, including homestead, arable land, and pasture, is twenty-nine hectares (Kinsey 1986). The Sabi River borders the area, while the Sengezi River runs through it, providing year-round livestock watering areas. The rearing of livestock, particularly cattle, is a significant source of income for many households. A fattened beast can fetch as much as $3,000 (1996 figures) from the private buyers who come directly to the villages to purchase animals and then resell them at a profit to the central Cold Storage Commission.

The resettlement office, Agritex office, veterinary services, and clinic are all located at a main resettlement centre. The core resettlement staff for these offices, plus primary school teachers, have their residences here. A row of dry goods and bottle stores are also located at the centre, as well as a carpentry and blacksmith operation run by a non-governmental organization. A primary school is nearby, and a secondary school is a few kilometres down the road; neither school has electricity or piped water. The resettlement centre has no electricity, but does have running water (most of the time), pumped by a generator. The settlers living next to this centre also have piped water at their homesteads, a luxury not shared by any other village in the scheme. The other villages have at least one borehole, but because these are frequently out of order, many settlers have dug wells.

The area is serviced by several bus lines, and most villages are within twenty kilometres of Wedza growth point, where goods can be marketed. However, settlers complain about transport problems, particularly the high cost of ferrying their maize to the Grain

Marketing Board (GMB) depot (the government-owned, centralized grain-buying facility in the country that sets prices and buys most of the grain produced by both small- and large-scale farmers). They also complain about the lack of electricity, which was promised to them by the government, and the lack of other infrastructural developments, such as dams. There are two irrigated areas in the Sengezi Resettlement; one benefits Village 4 and the other services a village not in the study sample. Villagers grow rape (a leafy green vegetable used to make the standard relish to accompany the staple food of *sadza*, a thick porridge made from ground white maize), tomatoes, beans, and maize on the irrigated land in the off-season, when they can get a good price for "green mealies," tender maize cobs that can be roasted or boiled and are considered a great treat. These irrigation schemes are highly successful and provide villagers with significant additional income.

Given these resources and conditions, and barring drought, resettlement families are able to live a rural life above a mere subsistence level. On average, however, they tend to be worse off than most people in communal areas. The reason for this is that although resettlement farmers generally earn more from farming than do communal area residents because of their larger arable fields, the major part of the communal area people's income comes from waged work. Most communal areas are "rural homes" for urban migrants with urban incomes, whereas resettlement farmers must exist primarily on farm income. The rule disallowing the migration of resettlement area household heads for reasons of employment is discussed in later chapters. Resettlement area households do rely to a certain extent on contributions from extended-family members, but these do not compare to the waged-work income in communal area households.

While communal area residents have relied on the input of migrant workers to survive, extensive unemployment and shrinking real incomes through the 1990s hit hard. Surveys by the Ministry of Agriculture show that poverty hits a third of all communal area dwellers and dire poverty affects about 10 per cent. Overall, the situation in resettlement is worse, with 41 per cent of the people defined as poor and 14 per cent as very poor.[21] Hence, comparing the living standards of communal and resettlement area dwellers requires more than comparing the size of arable land available to the average family. Wealth in communal areas is largely dependent on access to waged work, while farming success is central to resettlement areas. However, settlers in the Sengezi study site are relatively well off in comparison to settlers in many other resettlement schemes, particularly those that were initiated after the mid-1980s, when numerous constraints forced the government to restrict infrastructural and loan assistance, and those that lie in less viable farming regions.[22] Kinsey has been measuring poverty indicators in Sengezi and two other resettlement areas since 1983/84. He finds that while overall rates of poverty are worse in resettlement than in communal areas on a per capita basis, the larger household sizes with proportionally more younger members in resettlement areas mean an overstated rate of poverty in those areas. Since children consume less than adults and larger households are cheaper per member to operate than smaller households, poverty rates as measured by per capita expenditure do not fully capture the experience of poverty in resettlement. Kinsey finds that resettlement farmers are successful in making a living from farming, but are behind communal area farmers financially because they have access to fewer remittances and have more dependants in their households (Hoogeveen and Kinsey 2001).

To get a better sense of how to evaluate people's general living standards, I turn to definitions and standards of wealth. The four study villages, which I call Villages 1–4, have forty-one, forty-nine, fifty-five, and thirty-six households respectively. In spite of being allocated the same amount of arable land and being recipients of the same government schemes, such as seed loans and extension services, the villages are significantly differentiated by wealth. The settlers in the study site define wealth by number of cattle, agricultural yields, and the possession of agricultural implements. These form the bases of their livelihood and define their primary economic relationship to land. It is important to note that ownership of cattle represents wealth not only as a means of investment (i.e., future sale of cattle for cash) or savings (very important in inflationary economies such as Zimbabwe's), but also as a key component in agricultural production as draft power. A sketch of the level of material wealth of the people of Sengezi, the definitions of the four wealth groups or categories, and the percentages of households in the study villages that occupy these groups can be summarized as follows:

Group A: The wealthiest people are those with between ten and twenty cattle, a surplus of maize, farming implements like a plough, harrow, and scotchcart, and perhaps small livestock and other income-generating projects. About one-third of the households are identified in this group.

Group B: The second group has between three and ten cattle, grows a surplus of maize, but may have less farming equipment than Group A and may therefore have to borrow from people in the richest group. About 27 per cent of households fall into this group.

Group C: People in the third group have zero to three cattle and may or may not just grow enough maize for household consumption. They usually have to borrow farming implements. About 19 per cent of households fall into this group.

Group D: The poorest group usually has no cattle, does not usually produce enough maize for household food needs, and has no farming implements. This last group relies on help from wealthier families. About a fifth of households fall into this group.

From women's perspective, female-headed households form another important category. In the four study villages, nearly all of the "single" women with stands of land are widows; only one is divorced. In the latter unusual case, the husband left after the divorce and the stand fell to the woman. Divorce and remarriage are common occurrences, but divorced women normally move away and the husband retains claim to the stand. This means that, in this context, "female-headed household" nearly invariably means "widow."

Families were predominantly nuclear when they first arrived in the resettlement area. However, as the life cycle has progressed among settlers, the pattern has tended towards the building of extended families, with the original settlers as the heads. Average household size is 8.7 members, with a range from 4 to 19.

With respect to education, the survey of sixty households found that women farmers in the area have on average six years of formal schooling and male farmers around seven years on average. Nearly all the men and women we asked claimed to read Shona, and 59 per cent of the women and 73 per cent of the men said they could read English. This level of formal education means that employment options beyond general labourer are very limited.

All but seven people in the sample of sixty household representatives said they were Christians. About 38 per cent belonged to the older churches, Methodist, Anglican, or Roman Catholic, while close to half the sample belonged to one of the "new" churches, branches of the Apostolic Faith, Pentecostals, Seventh Day Adventists, and others. Altogether, nine different new churches were named. While the older religions have historically tolerated some aspects of traditional ancestral belief (such as rain-making ceremonies), many of the new churches distinguish themselves by banning ancestral appeasement and other ceremonies. In the sample, about half said they believed only in Jesus and not ancestral spirits and half said they believed in both or only in the ancestors. To make the situation even more complex, the people who say categorically that they believe only in Jesus and not in the ancestors sometimes respond to other questions in the interview as if they do believe in the ancestors. This religious complexity and its implications for gender and land are taken up in chapter 6.

Finally, I offer a brief word on community membership and dynamics. Wedza District saw a great deal of action in the protracted and bloody war of independence (Ranchod-Nilsson 1994). At the dawn of independence, residents of the district were not sure how to evaluate the government's resettlement plan. In the study site, there was initially extensive confusion about the purpose of being moved into the resettlement scheme. Recruitment of settlers was consequently difficult. Many people feared that they were being sent to do forced labour on the farms, as had occurred in the past. When these lands were owned by white commercial farmers before independence, people were often forced to work there if their cattle strayed onto the farms. According to a key informant, most of the first settlers were not volunteers but were chosen by their headmen in the communal area villages. These settlers formed three main groups. The first were the landless in the sense that they did not belong to lineage groups entitled to land in their village. The second group was made up of undesirable people, such as thieves and suspected witches. The third included individuals who had made leadership bids and were thus viewed as a threat to the incumbent headman. The members of all three groups were social outcasts. As mentioned in chapter 1, according to the district administrator, settlers were also drawn from among those who had been active in the war and were seeking land.

At first the settlers felt insecure about their claim to the land – partly because of the permit system (see chapter 3) – but by the 1990s settlers were treated as permanent residents. According to the settlers, the place belongs to them, largely because they do not have any other homes: "We take this place as our own because there is nowhere for us to go." They feel entitled to it because "we were given [it] by the government." It is common practice for people to bury their dead in the resettlement area rather than return them to *kumusha* (original home in communal lands). In part, this is for practical reasons (it is very far in some cases), but the act of burying the dead has important cultural implications as well (see chapter 6). Burying their dead in the resettlement area contributes to people's sense of ownership of the land: "Yes [it changes how we feel about the land] because we can't leave our dead here [i.e. the living could not leave the area after having buried people there], so we can't go anywhere."

The average distance to settlers' former homes is fifty-seven kilometres, a journey of one to two hours by bus depending on routes and connections. Only 18 per cent of the sample of sixty families live within reasonable walking distance from former homes (i.e., within five kilometres). While most families have maintained contact with their relatives in their original homes through visiting, they now view the resettlement area as their home.

The settlers in the four study villages come from many different original villages, although most of these are in Wedza District. The pattern of settling households from different lineages in the same resettlement village is a departure from customary settlement patterns (which are more homogeneous) and is socially significant in terms of the formation of local institutions and general social harmony (see chapter 6). The combination of a resettlement pattern that means settling with strangers (people of a different lineage) and the social outcast status of many of the settlers has produced a social context of suspicion, and accusations of witchcraft are common.

CONCLUSION

In all, the Sengezi Resettlement Area has good agricultural potential, relative land abundance, and residents who are struggling to find resources to bring that potential to fruition. With little formal schooling, residents have few options beyond farming. Socially, there are high levels of suspicion and households tend to act individually. There is totemic and religious diversity as well as significant wealth differentiation. Finally, as the population ages, the proportion of widows increases. We turn now to unravelling the situation for women and gender relations within this context.

3 Marriage and Land

"We share the fields so that the two of us have enough land to plough what we want differently."

This study, as well as others, shows that the single most important factor influencing a woman's relationship to agricultural land in resettlement is her marital status (see also Chenaux-Repond 1993; Jacobs 1991). Her status as a married, widowed, or divorced woman determines her social, cultural, and economic connection to the land, as well as the way in which institutional and ideological forces work to shape this gendered experience. For married women, who form the majority of women in resettlement, the institution of marriage functions from within and without the nuptial union to determine women's access to arable land. From without, resettlement policy dictates that a wife gains the right to farm in resettlement only because of her status as wife of a man granted resettlement permits (for cultivation, residence, and livestock pasturing). But these permits bear the man's name only. The married woman is therefore vulnerable to complete loss of land rights in the case of divorce. A permit holder may also be evicted for failure to comply with resettlement rules or for unacceptable social behaviour. Since a married woman has resettlement rights only through her husband, she is forced to leave the scheme if her husband is evicted, even if she has no part in the cause for eviction (Chimedza 1988). In Sengezi, eviction has been rare, but it still hangs over married women's heads as a structural danger.

This primary filtering of women's access to land is essentially conservative and follows common understandings of traditional practices in communal areas (see chapter 2). After this filtering, the state withdraws and leaves it up to the internal workings of the household to organize the allocation of land between husband and wife. Within marriage, gender ideology and custom mean that the husband generally decides on land allocation within the household. This chapter will thus now focus on how the internal dynamics of marriage affect resettlement women's access to and control of arable land and its produce. It also includes a discussion of other activities that married women pursue to generate income and examines how marriage affects these activities.

Marriage is also implicated in other aspects of the state's policy towards and treatment of women settlers. Some of these state practices have been positive for women, in some cases representing quite dramatic examples of gendered social change. These include treating women as farmers in their own right for training purposes and creating new household structures and dynamics through stipulations in resettlement policy. These aspects of state policy and their effects are discussed in chapter 4. In both chapters 3 and 4, I highlight the ways in which women negotiate and take advantage of spaces and dynamics to improve their lot, whether the opportunities lie in practices and ideologies labelled customary or traditional or in new areas opened up by progressive state policy. As found elsewhere, women "are using norms that empower them in other domains to gain access to land ... women contest and regain rights using the market, using kinship relationships, and using formal political and institutional structures" (Gray and Kevane 1999: 17).

MARRIAGE AND HOUSEHOLDS

As noted in chapter 2, in the Zimbabwean context, the nature of rural households has been profoundly shaped by the history of male migrancy and female subsistence farming. At a micro-level, rural households are characterized by gendered control of economic assets, including income, as well as by gendered economic responsibilities. These dynamics are consistent with feminist theory on households in Africa, which suggests that family members do not pool their income and that gender-specific expenditure is widespread. Women and men often hide their income from one another and spend it on different things (Fapohunda 1988: 147–50). One of the harshest aspects of this practice for women is that their husbands, by withholding money, may prevent them from meeting their economic responsibilities, such as feeding their children. Men control most income, whether it is their own wages or the money made through their wives' agricultural labour. Women's high degree of responsibility for subsistence farming and providing food for children limits their involvement in income-generating activities and reduces the likelihood of male income benefiting the family as a whole. In other words, when women are the ones primarily responsible for the basic needs of the family, men feel justified in spending a great deal of their income on themselves. This situation has been documented throughout the region south of the Sahara. Several decades ago, Murray (1981) noted this in Lesotho, as did Hay and Stichter (1984) for the region as a whole. Pankhurst and Jacobs (1988) provided evidence on this dynamic for Zimbabwe in the 1980s.

The story of a rash of suicides by women farmers in Zimbabwe following a bumper harvest in 1996 makes this point. On receipt of a large lump sum of money from the sale of grain, many husbands reportedly disappeared for several weeks of debauchery, returning home penniless. I quote at length from the coverage of the story by the local press:

Statistics from Karoi Police and hospitals in the district indicate that the joy of bumper harvest is frequently marred by suicides. Many husbands fall to the temptations of having a nice time on money earned from crops sales. The situation is sometimes so bad that some husbands squander thousands of dollars at growth points and rural service centers and return home with nothing to show for the family's toil.

The result ... was that scores of frustrated wives committed suicide. In some cases the husbands themselves also committed suicide after realizing their folly ...

... [A] woman farmer from Magunje said the behaviour of many husbands after harvest was frustrating. She cited a case where a certain farmer earned about $8000. He went to cash his cheque in Karoi but did not come back home for the next five weeks.

The wife was worried and made a lot of effort to find her husband but without success. She was later told that her husband was staying with a certain woman in Karoi. She located the woman but the husband beat up his wife and told her to go back home and wait for him.

The woman went back home without a cent and when the husband eventually came, he had squandered all the money. The family has no money for children's clothes and there was no capital to buy inputs for the next rainy season. The wife was so frustrated that she hanged herself and such cases are very common in this district. ("Bumper harvest triggers fear of suicides," *Sunday Mail*, 2 June 1996: 1)

In response to this story, the government issued a statement through Tenjiwe Lesabe, the minister of national affairs, employment creation and co-operatives (the ministry in charge of advancing the position of women), expressing dismay that women are sidelined in household decisions, particularly in the case of income earned through their own labour:

We must not tolerate these shameful acts of squandering the family's income. Harvest proceeds must be used within the family to buy food and other necessities. It must not be left up to wives/mothers only to think about family needs; it is indeed impossible for them to do so after fathers squander family resources ...

... Because women are the major contributors to agricultural production ... it only stands to reason that they should participate as such in agricultural decision-making. ("State of women suicides over harvests worry State," *Sunday Mail*, 16 June 1996)

The minister encouraged women farmers to register their own marketing card (the document identifying farmers who can sell produce to the Grain Marketing Board), so that cheques would come in their names, and to open their own bank accounts. She also supported the need for women to have primary access to land and for changes in inheritance laws to improve women's position.

The prevailing dynamic in rural areas, then, is of male control of most income, including income derived from the agricultural efforts of wives. Gender ideology grants male entitlement above and beyond male contribution. Women, on the other hand, are seen as responsible for the provision of basic necessities, especially food, for the family, but are often denied access to the means with which to do this. See Figure 3.1, a pictorial representation of this dynamic that appeared in the local press. Although this depiction is of an urban household, it reveals the same gender ideology. The woman asks her employed husband for money to buy the basic foodstuff, mealie meal. He

Figure 3.1
The Domestic Politics of Gendered Income
Source: Sunday Mail (Harare), 3 March 1996.

responds that she is lazy and should generate some income like other women. Meanwhile he sits at ease beside his stereo, drinking his eleventh beer. The cost of eleven beers was equivalent, at the time of the publication of the cartoon, to the cost of about twenty kilograms of mealie meal, enough for a family of four for a month. Some scholars have found that women in communal areas often devise secretive means to remove labour and resources from the realm of the household and patriarchal control, "in order to meet their needs and those of their children for cash income" (Pankhurst and Jacobs 1988: 212).

The household described here is clearly not an altruistic unit, with shared aspirations and goals among its members. Rather, the household is a productive location that is used by men to extract and control resources and income. Moreover, as noted, the productive activity required to sustain the wife and children often goes on outside the household, and thus even the concept of the household as an economic unit needs to be questioned in this context. While some men may use income and resources for the benefit of their families, it is more often the case that men use their power to the detriment of their wives and children, who survive in spite of their membership in a household, not because of it. Again, these dynamics support the arguments of some of the feminist literature on household economics (Guyer 1988; Folbre 1988).

The predominant gender dynamics of households in Zimbabwe are underpinned by patri-local customs and marriage practices. According to ethnographic accounts, in the norms of Shona marriage, a man gains rights to a woman's reproductive and productive labour through the payment of *lobola* (a marriage consideration) to the woman's patriarchal kin. This payment is seen as conferring status on the wife among her own kin and indicates the husband's family's gratitude and respect for the new wife (Bourdillon 1987; Weinrich 1979). In the ideals of tradition, a marriage is more a relationship between two family groups than a relationship between two individuals. As such, the marriage consideration, customarily made up of cattle, is drawn from the groom's father's herd and given to the bride's father. In turn, these cattle are often used as *lobola* for the marriages of the bride's brothers, giving her status among her own kin. In her married home, a bride has low status, being expected to do unpopular work for her mother-in-law and sisters-in-law. However, as she bears children, she gains status and rights to fair treatment; for example, she has the option to return to her natal home if she is mistreated or sexually unsatisfied (Bourdillon 1987).

In contemporary times, while these ideal norms may be only incompletely realized, they still carry moral weight, encouraging notions of "proper" gender and power relations in marriage. The payment of *lobola* is now predominantly a cash payment, and grooms are expected to earn the amount themselves through wage employment. The payment is made to the bride's father, who increasingly views it as personal income rather than as a fund to aid his own sons' marriages. Hence, marriage has become less a contract between two families and more a transference of male control of women from the father to the husband. As such, *lobola* confers less status on the bride. In fact, it is increasingly seen as deepening female dependency on a husband's goodwill, justifying a husband's unquestionable authority in the family in terms of decision making, control of resources, and the right to use violence to discipline his wife (or wives) and children (Bourdillon 1987; Weinrich 1979; Zinanga 1996).

Within this context of the supremacy of the husband, there are spheres of female autonomy and women do have access to and control over important resources. It is a customary practice, for example, for a husband to allocate his wife or wives a field from his own larger allocation. The wife customarily controls this field, know as *tseu*, on which she normally grows important supplementary foods such as peanuts, beans, or sweet potatoes, both for home consumption and for sale. Women historically have also cultivated gardens in riverine and wetland areas; such gardens are usually under their exclusive control. In a context where men control most of the household resources and income and women are responsible for supplying key family needs, it is crucial that women have access to and control over the resources and income that are seen as belonging to them. Over time, however, increased land pressure in colonial times in Tribal Trust Lands and the land use controls implemented through the Native Land Husbandry Act (NLHA) of 1951 have eroded the practices of *tseu* allocation and garden cultivation. Tseu allocation has also been eroded by a household preference to devote all available land to lucrative cash crops, which fall under male control. The NLHA banned cultivation in areas where women often had their gardens, such as stream banks and wetlands, and formalized individual rights to arable land in the name of male household heads (Bourdillon 1987; Moyo 1995). In one study of seven districts, the Zimbabwe Women's Resource Centre and Network (ZWRCN) interviewed groups of women who said that it was the norm to be given fields of their own (ZWRCN 1994b: 18). Yet another ZWRCN survey of 173 households found that only 23 per cent of women had the special land allocation (ZWRCN 1996:17). Another researcher found that only about a third of the women in her sample had access to the traditional *tseu* (Chimedza 1988: 43).

It is important to emphasize that these characteristics of households are not static but are constantly being defended and renegotiated, particularly under conditions of change. In the Gambia, for example, Schroeder (2001) found that there had been a significant reorganization of the patterns of gendered household incomes as a consequence of changes in the economy that favoured women's market gardening and hurt men's farming incomes. The resulting economic imbalance in favour of women led to complex social bargaining and symbolic manipulations wherein men found new ways to extract wealth from their wives. In the process, however, women won new types of autonomy and privilege: "Thus the product of lengthy intra-household negotiations brought on by the garden boom was not the simple reproduction of patriarchal privilege and prestige; it was instead a new, carefully crafted autonomy that carried with it obligations and considerable social freedoms" (Schroeder 2001: 102). As will be documented below, the new social conditions of resettlement in Zimbabwe operate much like the changes in the economy in the Gambia to provoke new types of intra-household negotiations around gendered income and resources.

MARRIAGE AND HOUSEHOLDS
IN RESETTLEMENT

In the resettlement process, it is left to the discretion of the husband to allocate portions of land to his wife or wives. In a sample of forty households in Sengezi, nearly two-thirds (65 per cent) said that the husbands allocated wives a field or fields. The Agritex worker holds the view that most men in the area allocate one or two acres to their wives, although a few farm the whole twelve acres (five hectares) together with their wives. The figure of 65 per cent is very close to the 60 per cent found by Chenaux-Repond's sample in resettlement areas (Chenaux-Repond 1993). She notes, too, that in the case of polygynously married wives, the granting of a field is not necessarily an advantage, as in some cases the husband excused himself from any additional contribution to her or her children in spite of her labour on his own fields. In her study, of those women who had not been given a field, some had asked for one and been refused and others had not bothered, a few because they intercropped their own crops in the husband's fields but most of them because they knew they would be refused. The husband was intent on utilizing all fields to maximum cash-cropping capacity (Chenaux-Repond 1993). Thus, the new situation of relative land wealth in resettlement did not guarantee women's access to the traditional *tseu*. Chenaux-Repond discovered that many men who wished to sidestep the custom of allocating fields to wives used the language of the permit to cultivate as justification. Section 5 of the permit to cultivate stipulates: "The holding shall be used solely for agricultural purposes, for the holder's exclusive benefit, and shall not be subdivided." While the wording of the permit was never intended to prevent men from allocating their wives fields, it has provided justification for some men inclined to deny *tseu* to their wives.

Another study of a small sample of wives on resettlement schemes found that most wives were allocated fields by their husbands (Chimedza 1988). Chimedza also points out that age is an important factor in the allocation of *tseu*, with older wives being more likely to have a field as well as greater decision-making power in the family. Jacobs's study (1991) concludes that resettlement wives are not less, and perhaps a bit more, likely to be allocated a field. However, her figure of 37 per cent of married women being allocated fields is very low compared to other findings. An interesting comparison can be made with the situation of wives in the small-scale commercial farms (formerly Native purchase areas). Cheater (1981, 1984) notes in her study of Msengezi that where holdings are on average between eighty and one hundred hectares, wives are usually allocated arable land well beyond what would be considered the traditional wife's portion. This land is still less than that granted to additional male farmers attached to the household, and most of the income deriving from a woman's labour is still appropriated by the husband. Nevertheless, women were able to earn enough money to buy clothes, schoolbooks, and so on, going beyond their traditional role of food providers.

Although the question of whether or not a wife is allocated a field is important in ascertaining her economic status, ending the enquiry at this point may miss some aspects of women's access to agricultural produce. In my study, there is some indication that some husbands have demoted their wives from the position of principle farmer to the status of labourer. As one woman says:

Wives are treated differently [from wives in communal areas] because some women they are not given the land or field to do whatever she wants; and the husband is the boss every time he shouts to the wife to wake up early to go to the field; after hard work the woman will come and work again at home; in communal areas the fields are smaller and the work is easier no matter the man is strict; here in resettlement we have more quarrels because we stay together, rather than in communal areas they have more love when the husband comes home from work [i.e., from town] because he just supervises and the woman is in charge.

My data thus lend some support to the view that the formal allocation of primary land rights to married men through the permit system can interfere with women's customary secondary rights to arable land, whether or not these rights are also being eroded by the economic incentive to grow more cash crops. The permit system also buttresses patriarchal control in the family by investing the husband with the only formal rights to land. However, the permit system does not necessarily decrease women's access to subsistence foods and income through crop production; it is important to dig deeper into the gender relations of crop production to ascertain whether or not this is true. Power and control reside not only in who has the stated right to a piece of land but also in who is said to control particular crops. Again, this is a distinction commonly relevant throughout the region: "There is a common story about women and land tenure status that transcends ethnic, cultural, and national boundaries in sub-Saharan Africa. The story begins by placing women not as 'owners of land' but rather as 'owners of crops.' Women generally have rights to cultivate land as well as rights to control income from resulting crop production" (Gray and Kevane 1999: 16).

MEN'S CROPS/WOMEN'S CROPS

Of a sample of forty households in Sengezi, all households said they grew maize and groundnuts (peanuts, Shona *nzungu*). Most grew rapoko (thirty-five households), roundnuts (bambara nuts or ground-peas, Shona *nyimo*) (thirty three households), sunflower (twenty-nine households), and beans (twenty-eight households). Other crops mentioned, but grown by fewer than ten households in the sample, were sorghum, cowpeas, rice, and sweet potatoes. Of these major crops, some are thought to be men's crops and some women's crops.

Maize is the major crop, providing the staple food and the biggest income. Groundnuts, roundnuts, rapoko, and beans are important household consumption foods, but surpluses are often sold. Table 3.1 shows data on gender relations in the six major crops. Women and men's views are disaggregated, revealing important gender splits in perceptions. The data reveal that women predominantly view maize as a man's crop. Men, however, are split on this, about half saying it is a man's crop and half saying it belongs to both the husband and wife or to the family in general. Similarly, more women than men state that beans are a man's crop, while men are more likely to say they belong to both men and women or to the family. A smaller such gender difference of perception exists in the case of sunflower, again with men more likely than women to say the crop belongs to the family. This gender gap suggests that women have a more rigid sense of what belongs to the man; perhaps they are more aware of how certain resources are beyond their control and of how men dominate the family. The men seem to have a more familial view of their own areas of control, revealing a type of patriarchal ideology that places them in control but asserts that this control is used for the benefit of the family at large. As male generosity may not always be forthcoming, it is important to document the areas of control that both women and men define as well respected.

In the case of crops, there is no gender split in perceptions concerning groundnuts and roundnuts, with most of the men and women agreeing that these are women's crops. What does the label "women's

Table 3.1
Gender Relations in Major Cropping Practices

Crop	Who decides what, where, and when to plant?	Men's Crops (%)	Women's Crops (%)	Both (%)
Maize	Women say (N = 20): *Men Joint Women** 70 25 5	90	5	5
	Men say (N = 20): *Men Joint Women Other*** 70 25 5	55		45
Groundnuts	Women say (N = 20): *Men Joint Women Other* 55 25 15 5		95	5
	Men say (N = 20): *Men Joint Women Other* 10 30 55 5		95	5
Rapoko	Women say (N = 18): *Men Joint Women Other* 61 28 11	67	11	22
	Men say (N = 17): *Men Joint Women Other* 65 35	59	5.5	35.5
Roundnuts	Women say (N = 20): *Men Joint Women Other* 50 20 30	10	85	5
	Men say (N = 14): *Men Joint Women Other*** 14 14 64 8			
Sunflower	Women say (N = 14): *Men Joint Women Other* 79 14 7	71	14.5	14.5
	Men say (N = 16): *Men Joint Women Other*** 63 31 6	69		31
Beans	Women say (N = 17): *Men Joint Women Other* 53 23.5 23.5	41	41	18
	Men say (N = 12): *Men Joint Women Other*** 34 50 8 8	25	8	66

* Refers to a female respondent who is a widow.

** Refers to one male respondent who followed an unusual practice in field allocation and cropping. He allotted his wife one-quarter of the total five hectares, keeping the rest for himself. On their respective portions, they both farm a large variety of crops, each making their own decisions about them and controlling the income therefrom.

crop" actually mean? The first column in Table 3.1 contains answers to the question "Who decides what, where, or when to plant?" From the responses, it is clear that there is significant male involvement in decisions around women's crops. In the case of groundnuts, for example, 55 per cent of women say that the man decides what, where, and when to plant the crop. In the case of roundnuts, 50 per cent of women make this claim. However, my study revealed that the dominant practice in the area is for women to control income from what are called women's crops. This has also been found elsewhere (ZWRCN 1994b: 18). In the case of men's crops, decisions about income are either taken by the man or in a process of discussion with his wife. From this, then, it can be argued that a woman's lack of a designated field or fields of her own does not necessarily mean that she lacks access to agricultural income from her crops. Only 65 per cent of the women and men in the sample said that wives were allocated fields, while a 100 per cent said they grow groundnuts, which in 95 per cent of the cases are to be the woman's crop. Roundnuts, also grown by most households in the sample, are designated mostly as a woman's crop. These findings support Chimedza's view that formal access to land is less crucial to women than is the control over the produce of the land (Chimedza 1988). In her study, Chimedza found that many women's crops were intercropped with maize, so that where maize is the dominant crop, male control of fields may not hinder women's access to women's crops.

In my case study, then, the permit system in resettlement, which gives married men exclusive primary rights to all arable land, has not necessarily decreased married women's access to and control of produce from the land; rather, the large increase of the size of arable land available to the household has led to an improvement in married women's opportunities to earn and control their own income, even though a large minority of women have not been allocated the traditional women's fields (*tseu*). The comments of a number of respondents indicate that the increased size of the fields in resettlement has meant that the families can now grow a greater number of crops; this has distinct advantages for women, as many of these are women's crops:

Yes, it's different because we now all want to plant different types of crops so we share the fields so that the two of us have enough land to plough what we want differently. (Woman Farmer A)

Yes, it's different, because here we have got enough land to grow our crops, crops for mother and father. (Woman Farmer B)

Further, when asked whether their situation as women has improved in any way since coming to the resettlement area, the majority of respondents mentioned having access to more income from more crops as a reason that their lives have improved. Hence, while women are still confined to an inferior position in regard to primary access to the main productive resource (arable land), they are better able to meet their goals of providing nutritious foods for their families and producing a surplus for sale that avails them of cash over which they generally have exclusive control.

OTHER FORMS OF INCOME GENERATION BY MARRIED WOMEN

Many women in the area have gardens, usually located in wetlands, on riverbanks, or, in one village thanks to piped water, at the homestead. Of the forty households interviewed on the topic, thirty-two have gardens operated by women. While some of these gardens produce foods only for domestic use, many others produce a surplus that is sold to other villagers, to teachers, to people in neighbouring communal areas, or at markets in the nearby town centres of Wedza or Marondera. Men, as well as women and children, are involved in the building of gardens. Further, men may help in the care of gardens, watering, spraying chemicals, and digging beds, although women and children are primarily responsible for the upkeep. Despite this male labour, the income from the sale of garden produce is strictly defined as belonging to women. (Donald Moore [1993] found that this is also the case with women's cultivation of *tsenza* [an edible tuber] in Kaerezi Resettlement Area in Nyanga District. Men may help plow the area for this crop, but that contribution in no way diminishes women's exclusive claim to the crop.) Of the thirty-two households interviewed with gardens, five said that there was joint control of the proceeds from sales, while two said that the man controlled the income. The remaining twenty-five households said that income from the garden was completely controlled by the woman. Most women also do the selling of the produce, although in the one case where the man did the selling, the income still belonged to his wife. Although the income is small compared to that available to men through cattle and crop sales, it is important to note the strength of the respect, from both men's and women's perspectives, that is accorded to women's right to this income.

A majority of the women interviewed on the topic operate income-generating projects of some kind. Apart from gardens, women also mentioned poultry feeding, sewing, and pottery making. It has been commonly observed that Shona women are entitled to the income earned and property obtained through their industry over and above their duties with regard to their husbands' land and domestic work. Known as *maoko* property (literally, "property of the hands"), the proceeds belong to women (Chenaux-Repond 1993).

Women are often involved in income generation or savings activities as a group. Of the twenty women asked the question, only two did not belong to a women's group, and this only because they had not been living in Sengezi long enough. Working in groups to generate income was also popular among women in colonial times. The Federation of African Women's Clubs, begun in the 1940s by European wives, fostered the establishment of local clubs to spread domestic skills such as sewing, proper hygiene, and "wifely propriety" among African wives in rural areas. The clubs spread rapidly in the 1960s and 1970s when the Rhodesian government turned to a "community development" strategy in the African reserves, after the failure of the Native Land Husbandry Act (1951) to improve peasant agriculture (see chapter 1). With the spread of the clubs, their nature changed as women rapidly turned their domestic skills to income generation and pressured the clubs to focus on adult education, literacy, and leadership skills (Ranchod-Nilsson 1992).

Many women are involved in savings clubs, each member contributing a set amount per week or per month and the members taking turns making use of the pot of money. Some of these clubs are national in membership, such as the "Self Help Development Group" started by Grace Mugabe, the second wife of President Mugabe. A joining fee goes to a provincial leader who then operates a rotating savings scheme. Women also mention the group activities of cattle fattening, poultry and pig fattening, sewing, and cooperative gardening. Women have also formed their own farming cooperatives, pooling their money to buy supplies in bulk and/or to "help each other with farming" in other ways. A woman from one village explained how a group of women had recently formed a farming cooperative "when they split from the men's farming union." With twelve members, the women "get money from selling their crops and bank some of the money." Clearly, women find that working as a group serves their interests. The fruits of group activities carry the protection of being *maoko* property and of being produced outside the confines of the household.

Jacobs (1991), too, found women's clubs to be important in her study of women in resettlement. Nearly all the villages in her study had established women's clubs whose predominant function was to foster women's income-generating projects, although in many cases the clubs also served as a forum for women to discuss personal problems, such as their relations with their husbands. I did not explore this aspect of clubs in my study, although in mid-1996 I discovered that women in the area were beginning to join a chapter of the Women's Action Group (WAG). WAG was formed in the early 1980s as a feminist activist group committed to legal change, women's land rights, and fighting violence against women. While its head office is in Harare, where it has a resource centre and publishes a bimonthly magazine (*Speak Out/Taurai/Khulumani*), its membership is predominantly rural. Members receive the magazine, plus other written information concerning women's health, women's legal status and rights, violence against women and children, and ways to resist traditional practices seen as oppressive to women, such as widow inheritance (a deceased husband's brother or other male relative marrying his widow). In the study site, leaders of the local WAG group said that WAG was "spreading like wildfire." They displayed their literature and explained how they hold discussion groups on topics such as inheritance, the importance of having a registered marriage to protect widowed or divorced women, non-sexist child-rearing practices (such as teaching both girls and boys domestic chores and granting daughters equal opportunities in education), and the importance of generating one's own income in order to be independent of one's husband and hence promote harmony in the household. They also discuss the need to change marriage traditions (abolishing *lobola*, for example) and the need to form "Men's Action Groups" to raise men's awareness of the desirability of such changes. Leaders of local chapters are invited to large workshops – such as the one held in 1996 at the University of Zimbabwe – to meet with leaders of other chapters and with the leadership of WAG, who have access to up-to-date information concerning legal and other policy changes around issues such as land reform. Women's groups could become a radical social force for change in gender relations, particularly if "consciousness" is accompanied by economic advancement and structural changes in the law and custom.

CONCLUSION

This chapter has outlined gender dynamics in the major livelihood arena of agriculture in a Model A resettlement scheme, as well as other important economic activities for women. Clearly, institutional structures limit women's opportunities to use the major resource of land and fundamentally affect the character of their relationship to land. The state plays a role in this through its imposition of a land use system (the permit system) that restricts women's primary access to land. History and culture have informed state policy in this respect, making the call for primary rights to land for women a formidable task for local and national women's groups.

Resettlement policy creates a situation wherein a married woman must rely on the largesse of her husband (he may be under some pressure from accepted practices) for an allocation of land to till. Evidence presented in this chapter indicates that, in this limited institutional context, important sites of female control and agency lie within the gendered relations, responsibilities, and entitlements of households. Women's crops and robust boundaries around certain types of women's income form an important material base for women's lives as economic beings. Women have been quick to maximize and protect these areas of autonomy. However, this is only part of the story. Chapter 4 identifies other areas of opportunity and constraint in relation to the more direct effects of state policies and agents.

4 Married Women, the State, and Family Dynamics

"... they have to go together to cash the cheque"

INTRODUCTION

In chapter 3, it was shown that through the practice of allocating permits to husbands only, the state plays a conservative role, mirroring similar practices in communal areas and hence placing limits on married women's access to arable land. In this chapter, the focus shifts to an examination of aspects of state policy and treatment of married women that have provided opportunities and spaces for women. These state actions can be attributed to the state's somewhat positive position towards some aspects of gender equity (now severely eroded) in the early years of independence (see chapter 2). These state practices are divided into two main categories. The first are those in which state agents treat women as farmers or settlers in their own right, extending training opportunities and membership in special projects to married women as individuals. The second are less direct and involve the gendered effects of state policy on household structure and internal dynamics. Most important here is the state's insistence that husbands remain on the resettlement stand with their wives and operate as full-time farmers. This policy swims against the norm in communal areas, from which most married men migrate for waged work, and hence creates new household forms and internal dynamics. Also of interest are the effects of the resettlement process on rates of polygyny and extended family structures and relationships.

WOMEN AS FARMERS

According to one of the Agritex workers I interviewed, women are the main farmers in the area. They outnumber men at his extension meetings and form three-quarters of the members in his master farmer classes. While men are around, they "lag behind," he says. Some men do piecework in neighbouring commercial farms, leaving women to do the main farming on resettlement.

There are profound implications for the control of the major income in the household when the woman has a master farmer certificate. First of all, the woman's name can appear on the cheque from the Grain Marketing Board (GMB), where the major cash crops, such as maize, are sold. A key informant in the area (the acting head of the local high school) explained that because of outstanding debts, many men were finding large chunks of money automatically deducted from their GMB cheques, and thus, around 1993, they came up with the idea of having their wives registered as the master farmer so that the cheque would come in her name. Since the wives have no registered debts, nothing would be deducted. The men then come with their wives to the school post office to collect the cheques: "But don't think," said one of the men, "that this is not my money. It is still mine although it's got my wife's name on it!" However, it is true that this system may help keep husbands from such practices as wasting the entire cheque on long binges. As the local high school head master reports, "Having the cheques in the woman's name helps this because they have to go together to cash the cheque. The woman can have more say. We don't have such men here. They give most of the money to the wife who gives them maybe $20 to get drunk then he comes back sober the next morning. Men don't disappear for five or six days around here."

As mentioned in chapter 3, women have formed their own farming cooperatives. They are also involved in some activities usually associated with men, such as cattle fattening. It has been found elsewhere that the permit system jeopardizes women's commonly accepted right to keep some cattle. Generally, in Shona society, while men own most of the cattle, it is considered traditionally proper for women to receive a cow on the marriage of a daughter. Women may also inherit cattle from their own mother or other female relatives. These cattle may be increased through breeding. In the resettlement context, however, like the permit to cultivate, the permit to put stock to pasture normally bears the name of the husband. Any stock that women have, therefore, must be incorporated into the total allowed to the permit holder. Chenaux-Repond found that only a fifth of wives in her study owned cattle and 27 per cent owned goats. Men permit holders said that they intended to ask their wives to send stock to their parents in the communal areas if their own stock reached the permit limit (Chenaux-Repond 1993). According to the resettlement officer, this is also the likely pattern in the Sengezi Resettlement.

In my study, men dominate in the buying and selling of cattle, but women are undertaking commercial cattle raising in their own right in the area, hence challenging traditional norms and sidestepping a disadvantage of the permit system. Cattle rearing is not only a means of wealth accumulation, but also a deliberate income-generating activity. Private buyers and the Cold Storage Commission (the central meat board of the country) hold local auctions where farmers can sell beasts on the spot for cash. A large beast can fetch as much as $3,000 (at 1997 prices), or the equivalent of five or more months' pay at a low-skilled job in town. The Agritex worker offers technical information on feed, dosing, and preferred breeds for fattening. A donor agency, Christian Care, has initiated some group cattle-feeding projects. One of these groups is made up of fifteen women, who had sold about fifteen beasts by mid-1996. The Agritex worker states that men tend to work individually in cattle feeding, while few women work on their own in this occupation. Although women have often kept a small number of cattle, their involvement in cattle rearing as an income-generating activity marks a big change in their conventional sources of income. This change has been encouraged by the outside interventions of a donor agency, as well as by a state representative, the Agritex worker.

Women are also involved in their own right in one of the major money-making ventures in the resettlement, irrigation. There are two irrigation schemes in Sengizi, one funded by the Dutch government and located in one of the study villages, and the other a government project and located in a village not in the study. Both schemes fall under the supervision of the Agritex worker, who allocates the plots and provides advice on crop selection and farming practice. The participating farmers grow cash crops such as green maize, leafy vegetables, onions, tomatoes, potatoes, and beans. The Agritex worker is also trying to introduce wheat, which, though difficult to grow, would earn higher returns. The produce is marketed in the nearest town centres, but transportation is a problem. Some of the plots are allocated to the "family," but some are taken by women in their own right, even by some married women. According to the Agritex worker, in a family, a husband, wife, and son can all have their own plots, although this leads to shortages of seeds, fertilizer, and so on. The Agritex worker, as a gatekeeper to one of the main income-generating opportunities in the resettlement, has clearly accepted women as farmers in their own right, entitled to partake in a major project as individuals. What emerges is a sense that women have considerable identity as farmers in their own right in the area, as a result both of the enlightened attitude of state officials such as the Agritex worker and of new ways major income from agriculture is controlled in the household, at least partly because of women gaining master farmer certificates. This is reflected in the profile of household decision-making and spending practices discussed in the next section.

HOUSEHOLD FORMS AND DYNAMICS

As discussed in chapter 3, income marked as women's income is predominantly viewed as immune to claims from or negotiations with other household members. This is not the case for income marked as men's income. While major sources of income, such as that from maize and cattle sales, are seen as dominated by men, most of the people in group interviews (N = 9 gender-segregated groups, of four to nine people each) said either that husbands and wives should make joint decisions about men's income or that the wife should have some say in the decisions.

Further, there is a strong tendency for men to be named as responsible for earning the money for major household expenditures. School fees are said to be only or mostly men's responsibility, although working children and wives can "help." Even stronger is the sense that men are responsible for earning money for farming implements, with all groups saying this is a duty for men only. Less strong but still predominant is men's responsibility for household needs like soap and cooking oil, with four groups of the nine saying that women were mostly or exclusively responsible. The responsibility of paying for furnishings such as beds, lounge suites, tables, benches, and so forth was more strongly gendered, with seven groups saying this was mostly or only men's role, while four groups said that women sometimes contributed or that both men and women were responsible for these expenditures.

It appears that the ideology surrounding gendered economic responsibility in the household roughly matches the unequal control of income sources. This is unlike the situation of women farmers married to migrant men described in chapter 3, where men control most of the income, while women shoulder most of the responsibility for the family needs. While income-earning opportunities and decision making are still gendered in a way that affords women less power than men, the prevailing moral code is that men should use this greater power for the betterment of the family. From the data here, it appears that men generally take on major responsibilities in the maintenance of the household. This supports Jacobs's finding that women say that husbands and wives work together as a unit in resettlement and that wives share in major decision-making processes. Their influence appears to have increased in comparison to norms in communal areas, although there is still marked power inequality (Jacobs 1991). This may be in part a result of the surveillance of local officials, namely the resettlement officer, who keeps watch over men to ensure that they reinvest their money in farming and do not neglect their families (Jacobs 1991). As shall become clear in chapters 5 and 7, however, this apparent climate of shared economic responsibility in households is severely compromised by the threat and frequency of male infidelity and divorce. Therefore, while the norm for married couples may be somewhat more congenial from women's point of view as compared to that in communal areas, this improvement must be contextualized within the broader pattern of marital instability.

Another aspect of household structure to be considered is the question of polygyny. Some scholars have drawn parallels with the situation in the small-scale commercial farms (formerly Native purchase areas – see chapter 1), wherein polygyny has been the major strategy to harness enough labour for the large farms (Shutt 1995; Cheater 1981; Bourdillon 1987; Weinrich 1979). The argument suggests that the overall trend in resettlement has been for men to treat wives as labour in the household production unit and consider themselves the sole holder of land use rights and the sole benefactor from the sale of crops. This has led, it is argued, to increases in rates of polygyny in resettlement where ethnic groups favour this practice (Chenaux-Repond 1993; Jacobs 1991). Rates are not as high as in small-scale commercial farms but higher than in communal areas (Jacobs 1991). Jacobs found a rate of 27 per cent in her sample from several schemes, while Chenaux-Repond found that overall 17.3 per cent of the married men were in polygynous unions, although in one scheme the rate was 35.3 per cent of all marriages. The average rates for Shona society are difficult to determine. Jacobs (1991) estimated that about 10 per cent of marriages in rural Shona society are polygynous, while the 1982 census estimated that the rate could be as high as 17.8 per cent of all marriages (Chenaux-Repond 1993). According to Chenaux-Repond's study (1993), many men who were polygynous when they settled subsequently married more wives, often making it clear that this was for the purpose of gaining more labour, and many men who were monogamous when settling subsequently became polygynous.

These trends are not found everywhere. In Sengezi the incidence of polygyny is almost non-existent. Out of a total of 181 households in the sample frame of four villages, only five husbands had two wives (2.8 per cent) and one (0.6 per cent) had four. In the village discussion groups, the men stated that these low rates were due not to men being culturally averse to the practice, but to a lack of the funds needed to marry another wife. Village women, however, like women all over contemporary Zimbabwe, dislike the practice. One comprehensive study states that 95 per cent of the women interviewed disapproved of polygyny (ZWRCN 1995).

The low rates of polygyny in Sengezi may be attributable to factors other than lack of funds. The scheme studied is relatively successful, and hence relative poverty cannot be the reason that rates here are so much lower than in the schemes studied by Jacobs and Chenaux-Repond. The main reason for low rates of polygyny in Sengezi may be that the main cash crop, maize, is much less labour intensive than the cotton and tobacco grown on Chenaux-Repond's study sites, a connection also made by Chenaux-Repond.

Jacobs (1991) found that the meaning of "family" in her study of resettlement was the nuclear core. This represents a change from the situation in communal areas, where people tend to settle close to others of their lineage and participate in a wide extended-family network. In Jacobs's study, both men and women expressed satisfaction with the changed situation, seeing the extended family as oppressive and interfering. This shift in the meaning of "family" is linked to an increased sense of individualism. This finding challenges a tendency in Western feminist theory (with roots in Engles's 1902 *The Origin of the Family, Private Property and the State*) to see the nuclear family as

oppressive to women. The nuclear family historically has been seen
to intensify the private nature of the domestic sphere, making
women's domestic and productive work invisible and undervalued
and, with the family cut off from public and extended-family censure,
providing a more conducive place for domestic violence. The nuclear
family also cuts women off from the support of the extended family,
such as with child care. Chimedza (1988) makes this latter point with
respect to the nuclearization of the family in resettlement. Are families
and households predominantly nuclear in resettlement?

The families were predominantly nuclear when they first arrived
in resettlement. With the passage of time, however, the pattern has
tended towards the building of extended families, with the original
settlers as the heads. In my sample of sixty households, only 46 per
cent are composed of a husband, wife, and their unmarried children
or the unmarried children of relatives, such as nephews or nieces. In
about a fifth of the sample, mothers and father live with their grown
married children and their grandchildren. A slightly smaller proportion also include adult relatives, such as a mother or sibling of the
husband or wife, plus possibly their children in addition to the settler
couple's own children. Out of the seven widows in the sample, only
one lives alone with her unmarried children, while the others live
with at least one married daughter and a son-in-law, plus their children. There is one widower in the sample (he lives with his unmarried children) and there are two polygynous households composed
of three generations (wives, married children, and their children).
Average household size is 8.7 members, with a range from 4 to 19.
These household characteristics are very similar to those found by
Chenaux-Repond (1993). Also, as in her study, I found a strong tendency, contrary to cultural norms, for married daughters as well as
sons to stay on the family stand. This is probably due to the avail-
ability of enough land on the stand to feed a large family and few
employment or alternative farming opportunities elsewhere for
grown children. In this sense, there could be a tendency in resettlement away from small-scale commercial farming and towards subsistence as plots are subdivided to accommodate married children.
Indeed, the resettlement officer stated that while the subdivision of
plots is technically not allowed, in practice he does not interfere,
leaving it as a "domestic issue." The Agritex worker agrees. He said
that the informal subdivision of plots to give fields to grown sons
is common; indeed, the separate cribs of maize can be seen in the
homesteads. Subdivision may increase land productivity, but it

decreases the amount of income for each nuclear family. As the resettlement officer mentioned, since sons have to go through the regular channels in applying for a plot of their own, there is a strong tendency to subdivide. As the settler families progress through their life cycles, family structure expands from the nuclear core, creating new loci for extended-family formulation. With married daughters also remaining behind, there may in time also be implications for patrilineal control of land (see chapters 5 and 6).

In Sengezi, there is a discernible tendency towards focusing most resources on the family members who live on the resettlement stand, but the extended-family structure incorporating family living elsewhere is still very strong. Back and forth visiting between relatives has remained quite frequent, in spite of significant distances between the resettlement and people's original homes. The main reasons for these visits are funerals, traditional ceremonies, and just visiting. A few people mentioned that they visit their relatives in communal areas in order to help them, either with labour, clothes, or food. Indeed, a popular explanation given for relatives' visits to the settlers in resettlement was that they needed help, especially with food. Here are some examples:

They do visit us if they need something. (Woman Farmer 44)

They usually come in summer season because they want to eat some crops such as maize. (Woman Farmer 12)

They come in winter when they will be short of mealie-meal. (Male Farmer 19)

When the sample of sixty were asked if their responsibilities to their extended family would increase if they increased their own income through farming, only eight said that they would not increase their help to relatives:

We do not give it to our relatives, but we look after our family with the money. (Female Farmer 20)

I would help them a little but use the money mostly to develop my family. (Male Farmer 27)

In addition, almost half of the households support someone not living in the household. Besides children either at school or grown up and living in town, these dependants include parents, brothers, sisters, and even uncles of the resettlement couple. Also, nearly half of the households receive contributions from a family member who is in waged work. Most of these helpers contribute at least once a month, and some more often, with money, groceries, clothes, and school fees. The overall sense is that the ties and reciprocal obligations to extended family are still very strong.

Further, although the settlers in my sample have come from a wide variety of original homes, many of them have relatives living in the resettlement area, though not necessarily in the same village. Of these, most say that mutual aid with the extended family in resettlement is of a better quality than that among extended family in the communal areas.

This discussion makes it clear that households in resettlement are not predominantly nuclear, either in their actual structure or in the sense of there being hard boundaries restricting the flow of resources and mutual aid towards and from the broader extended family. Resettlement families help and are helped by their extended families. Given this, it is difficult to relate the nuclearization of the resettlement household to changes in women's status or position as Jacobs attempts. A much more definite change is the cohabitation of spouses.

One of the rules governing settlers in Model A schemes is that the permit holder must reside on the stand and engage in full-time farming. The purpose of this rule is to ensure that permit holders utilize the land to the fullest possible extent. The resettlement program is meant to boost the small-scale farming sector's contribution to the national agricultural yield as well as work towards greater land equity in racial terms. The rule is meant to prevent the development in resettlement of the communal area pattern that sees male household heads migrating to towns to work while women stay behind as the principal farmers.

Given this, the case of Model A resettlement provides starkly different family and gender dynamics for rural peasant farmers in Zimbabwe. Resettlement can be seen not only as a project for land redistribution and increased productivity, but also as a social project designed to provide a context for the cohabitation of spouses and a change in the gender relations of farming. As Jacobs puts it, the project may be a way of "effeminizing subsistence agriculture and of restoring it to its 'rightful' owners" (Jacobs 1984: 48). Since most of the permit holders are married men, resettlement provides a new type of social context for rural peasant households where men and their wives live and farm together. Chenaux-Repond found that this rule of resettlement was followed in her study schemes, where very few men had left the scheme to work elsewhere. I found the same thing in Sengezi. Only an insignificant number of permit-holding men had left the scheme for work reasons, and this is in spite of the fact that the resettlement officer had turned a blind eye to male migration since the implementation of ESAP (Economic Structural Adjustment Program) and the devastating drought of 1992, as it was recognized that economic hardship had become profound in many households.

For the most part, then, male permit holders are living and farming on the scheme, taking a much more active role in farming than is predominantly the case in communal areas. Although women are still the main farmers (see comments of the Agritex worker above), men are definitely involved, being primarily responsible for ploughing, making contours, stumping the fields, and cultivating with hoes and oxen. Women do the weeding and planting, and share in the work of driving oxen and applying fertilizers. Harvesting is also done mainly by women and children, but men are usually in charge of winter ploughing, constructing granaries, and transporting the harvest from the fields. Women tend to thresh their women's crops, but they can also be involved with men in threshing maize. Men dominate in the weighing, packing, loading, and marketing of maize. It is likely that the sharing of farm work leads to more sharing in decision making and household responsibilities (Jacobs 1991). Study participants reported that while women are predominantly in charge of the care of children, men in the study site take some responsibility for child care, such as by taking them to the clinic or traditional healer and paying for any necessary medication. This point was corroborated by clinic staff.

CONCLUSION

The gendered household responsibilities that accompany gendered incomes do not necessarily work against women, as men appear to accept a major portion of economic responsibility along with their control of most of the income. This more cooperative household dynamic appears to have multiple causes, including cohabitation of spouses and the unforeseen effects of such male initiatives as sending wives to master farmer training in order to escape indebtedness.

Other influences can be attributed to the state, such as the effects of progressive views of women held by state officials and the overall surveillance that makes it incumbent upon men to act responsibly as husbands and farmers in order to maintain the right to stay on the scheme. While feminist analyses have been locally criticized for investing too much hope in state change (Moyo 1995), the state has clearly played a major role in improving women's opportunities by treating women as farmers in their own right, granting them access to irrigation schemes and supporting their cattle-fattening projects. This theme is revisited in the next chapter, which discusses the advantages of state policy for widows in resettlement.

The state may have power to influence social change in some arenas, but may make little headway elsewhere. This is evident in the way extended families have developed in resettlement and in the resultant subdivision of arable plots, despite state dictates against it. There is also extensive contact between resettlement dwellers and extended family elsewhere, both in terms of giving and receiving aid. Therefore, resettlement does not appear to promote the nuclearization of households. This being the case, it is difficult to make inferences about nuclearization and women's status in resettlement. In terms of polygyny, it appears that factors beyond the mere fact of resettlement are responsible for increases in polygyny, the major factor being the type of major cash crop grown. Given the success of some state resettlement policies in protecting some of women's interests, it is possible that a state stand against polygyny would have some effect.

Feminist analyses of resettlement and land reform use predominantly structuralist and materialist analyses. These emphasize women's disadvantaged position as a result of gender-blind or gender-biased government policy and persistent social and cultural norms that leave women in subordinate positions with regard to access to and control of land. Feminist analyses also rely heavily on an argument based on the value placed on agricultural productivity, pointing out that since women are the main agricultural producers, it is counterproductive and inefficient to deny them full access to and control of land (ZWRCN 1994b; Pankhurst and Jacobs 1988). These approaches lead to the proposing of solutions that focus predominantly on the need to change structural conditions, such as state policy and laws.

Structural conditions are undoubtedly central in shaping the opportunities and constraints that women face in resettlement. My own data support a materialist perspective that emphasizes access to and control of economic resources, as well as a focus on how political, economic, and cultural conditions limit women's room to better their lives. However, I have also found important spheres of agency for women in prevailing gender relations. These include women's control of certain crops and market gardens, certain types of property and income that belong to women (discussed in chapter 3), the changing of gender ideologies as a direct result of enlightened state policy, and changes in gender relations at the micro-level of spousal couples that indicate more cooperative decision-making processes and a more equitable sharing of family responsibilities than appears to prevail in communal areas (as discussed in this chapter). An overly structuralist position that focuses only on women's disadvantaged position regarding primary access to land is unlikely to capture these important advantages for women and the highly dynamic social context within which they are generated; moreover, such a position fails to highlight the dexterity and acumen with which women seize opportunities to improve and protect their position. While the social system clearly subordinates women through mediating their economic rights through the institution of marriage, marriage does not deprive them of all economic rights or of all room to negotiate an improved sharing relationship within marriage.

Nevertheless, as shall become clear in chapters 5 and 7, women's primary vulnerability is indeed related to marital status. The worst thing that can happen to a woman, however, is not marriage, but divorce. In the next chapter, we begin the discussion of how divorce shapes women's lives, but we focus primarily on another group of women without men – widows.

5 Women without Men

"She will be acting as the father so that some people cannot see the difference."

"She was beaten and he tied both her legs and hands and threw her into the lorry."

INTRODUCTION

This chapter continues the discussion of the effects of state policy and actions in the lives of resettlement women, as mediated through their marital status. The resettlement system opened up some new opportunities for unmarried women to access land. Some resettlement permits were granted to widowed or divorced women with dependants in their own right. State policy has also supported the succession to permits of women widowed in resettlement schemes. This chapter focuses on the institutional dynamics affecting these women without men in Sengezi and examines some of the ideological contestation and negotiation surrounding their experiences.

WIDOWS AND DIVORCED WOMEN

In the early years of resettlement, as part of its early support for gender equity, the government was committed to a policy of allowing unmarried (that is, widowed or divorced) women with dependants to obtain permits for resettlement in their own right. This policy is a major advance for women, as it represents the unusual phenomenon of women having primary rights to agricultural land. However, over the years, only a small proportion of permits have been issued to women in this category. Another study of three resettlement schemes found that 11.6 per cent of permit holders were widowed or divorced women, a proportion of whom had become widowed after resettlement (Chenaux-Repond 1993). As discretion is given to the District Council and the Resettlement Office in the screening process, the proportion of single women to be granted permits depends in large part on the inclinations of these bodies. Countrywide, by 1988 only 7 per cent of permits were allocated to unmarried women (Fortmann and Bruce 1993).

As discussed in chapter 1, shifts in resettlement policy have increasingly tightened the criteria for resettlement eligibility in ways that have emphasized productivity and efficiency over social justice aims. Such shifts generally disadvantage single women applicants, as they have access to fewer resources and historically have not tended to receive farmer training. Such effects can be predicted from the policy changes regarding the criteria for resettlement selection implemented in 1992. Settler applicants are awarded a series of points based on farming skill, agricultural implements, education, and perceived need for the land, as well as a large number of points for the qualifications of a spouse of the permit applicant; thus, single-parent households are disadvantaged (Chenaux-Repond 1993).

In the Sengezi Resettlement, only three stand holders are divorced women (out of a total of 443 stands). We interviewed these three women, whose stories are recounted below. The remaining women permit holders are widows, about a third of whom joined the scheme as widows, while the rest became widowed after joining the scheme as married women. Thirty-nine of these widows were interviewed, several of whom are from different villages than the core four of the study; many of their stories are incorporated in what follows. Twenty women and twenty men in the four core villages were interviewed about the issues of women's experiences as widows and divorced women.

In Sengezi, both the resettlement officer and the district administrator for Wedza claim that the new selection criteria actually make it easier for single women with dependants to be granted land. This is because it is now easier for women to get master farmer certificates, an important element of the criteria, and allowances are made for the absence of a spouse. The former minister of lands and water development echoed this position at a land conference held in 1997. The minister stated that the ministry was not gender biased in that it would accept female applications for resettlement land. Further, the ministry was gender sensitive in that it would take into account the historical disadvantages faced by women that may cause them to appear less qualified than men in terms of educational status or ownership of farming implements. Since the ministry is aware that women are often the most experienced and skilled farmers, special allowances will be made in regard to selection criteria in order to favour female applicants.[1]

While this sounds hopeful, it remains at the level of unwritten policy. There are no imposed quotas or other specific directives to ensure that unmarried women will be granted resettlement land. These women will remain largely vulnerable to the perspectives of district administrators, resettlement officers, VIDCOS (Village Development Committees), and councillors, who control the flow of information about available resettlement stands, as well as the final selection of settlers.[2]

WIDOWS AND THE PERMIT SYSTEM

Readers will recall from chapter 1 that resettlement land belongs to the state and that settlers are granted only usufruct rights through the permit system. As such, stands are not inheritable. However, the resettlement authority has formulated a policy on the succession to permits upon the death of the permit holder. Unwritten government policy has been that widows in resettlement are allowed to stay on the plot if the husband dies and the permits and registration book are changed to bear her name (Chenaux-Repond 1993). In practice, this is often what transpires, including in Sengezi. Given the aging of the first generation of settlers and the fact that husbands tend to die before their wives, the incidence of widowhood on resettlement is becoming quite high. In the four core villages in my study, for example, widows head an overall 19 per cent of households. In one village, widows head a third of all households and hence represent a significant social group.

A widow succeeding to the permits represents a marked improvement in her status as compared to the usual practice in communal areas. Common practice in rural areas is that a brother or other male relative of the deceased husband takes over the care and management of the estate of the deceased. Frequently, the widow is expected to marry a brother of the deceased, especially if she is still of childbearing age. If a male heir is old enough to manage the estate, then it is passed to him. In theory, whether passed to a brother, other male relative, or the male heir, the estate is supposed to be used for the benefit of the widow(s) and the dependants of the deceased. In practice, however, the decades before independence in 1980 saw an increasing tendency for the relatives of the deceased husband to plunder his estate and evict the widow(s), often leaving her or them destitute. Post-independence legal reforms designed to change this situation in favour of widows have yet to yield significant results (Stewart 1992; Moyo 1995). Furthermore, recent rulings by the Zimbabwean Supreme Court (see chapter 2) that favour an interpretation of inheritance rights from the perspective of customary law rather than common law do not provide an encouraging legal context for widows.

The practice of resettlement stands being given to widows of deceased permit holders is well known in Sengezi. Both men and women are aware of it and say it is the dominant practice in their area. On the issue of rights to the fields, all female respondents said that a widow has the right to plough in the fields: "She will do what she wants on the use of fields because they will now be hers" (Female Farmer 18); and "It will belong to her and change the name from his to hers" (Female Farmer 31). For the most part, the responses of males are basically the same, reflecting the widow's control of the land: for example, "She takes on from where the husband left in looking after the children; she would be the only one responsible for the ploughing of the fields" (Male Farmer 7). Some men, however, retain more of the flavour of traditional practice in their answers. For example:

The widow looks after the children, that is if no one has inherited her; some who might be young go back to the parents; widows control everything with the help of the eldest son. (Male Farmer 34)

If she has got three or more children then she stays with the children, while if she has got only one child she can go if she wants; she takes on the services of her husband until the eldest son is mature enough to look after the family. (Male Farmer 47)

These types of responses from a minority of men suggest that while women are unanimous about the new practice in resettlement, there are still men around who are attached to the practices that see a widow's rights as mediated through the eldest son or a brother of the deceased. The same difference, although less strongly stated, appears in the responses regarding the widow's right to stay at the homestead. All of the women said that the widow has the right to stay at the homestead, making statements like the following: "She will be acting as a father so that some people cannot see the differences because she is the one left at home" (Female Farmer 33); and "She will live with the children; if the brother of the deceased comes talking nonsense she will talk to the resettlement officer" (Female Farmer 15).

The dominant theme in men's responses is the same: "She deserves the right to rule the family and decide how to run it" (Male Farmer 38). But some men have the view that the eldest son or one of the deceased's brothers should have a say: "The eldest son looks after the family" (Male Farmer 44); and "She is helped by the elder brother of the deceased or the younger brother" (Male Farmer 35). Indeed, it is interesting to note that many of the widows I interviewed said that they had "washed their son's hands" at the inheritance ceremony of their deceased husbands, a gesture that indicated their refusal to be inherited by a relative and have their son named as heir and new head of the family. While this practice is apparently increasing throughout Zimbabwe (Bourdillon 1987: 51), the context of resettlement is different in that this choosing of the son goes together with the changing of the name on the permits to that of the widow.

A similar gender gap in perception is reflected in the 71 per cent of women who said that land would be "inherited" by the widow and the only 54 per cent of men who said that this would happen (N = 60). These responses indicate that while the government policy of allowing widows to remain on the stands is widely practised and accepted in the study site, the issue appears to be somewhat conflictual. Given the differential power of men in the family and the culture, it is unlikely that customary practice could be changed without the intervention of the state. It also appears that the granting of succession rights to widows in resettlement influences inheritance practices regarding moveable property, such as furniture, and decreases the pressure for widows to marry a brother of the deceased. All twenty women interviewed on the question said that the widow has the right to all furniture and dishes in the homestead, except for the dead husband's clothes, which should be shared among his relatives. Most men interviewed (N = 20) said much the same thing, although they placed more emphasis on the use of household contents for the benefit of the family than on their use for the benefit of the widow per se. When women and men were asked whether any of these practices differed from practices in their former homes in communal areas, a significant number said that the practices were different. They referred mainly to the practice of widow inheritance, but also to the practice of sharing the property among the husband's relatives. Here are examples of typical responses:

SOME WOMEN'S VOICES:
It is different because at our communal areas you are forced to be remarried; they will be jealous if you take another husband who is not the brother of the deceased; here it is our land, the two of us, so I remain here; no one will come and give me rules. (Female Farmer 15)

There is a difference because in the communal areas if the husband is gone, the relatives of the man then send back the woman to her parents and they take over the place and property. (Female Farmer 19)

SOME MEN'S VOICES:
It is different because in communal areas you are forced to be remarried to the brother of the deceased because you will be in their homestead, but here in the resettlement, it's our land as two of us, no brother, no sister, so we do what we want. (Male Farmer 12)

It is not the same because here our land is controlled by the government so we use rules that are imposed by them, whereas in communal areas they use rules that were made by the forefathers. (Male Farmer 3)

Significantly, the sentiment captured by the phrasing "Here it is our land, the two of us / it's our land as two of us" is used by both men and women in resettlement, pointing to an overall agreement between men and women on a fundamental difference in landholding patterns between resettlement and communal areas.

Mrs R.'s name was put on the resettlement permits after her husband's death in 1992. She describes the behaviour of her deceased husband's brother:

He came asking for the permits. He asked kindly, saying that he wanted to pay the last payments of the stand. I refused politely. He came again as a kind person, wanting to help me in the fields. I refused politely. He came again, wanting to take the cattle to look after in the communal area. I refused. He came again with groceries and he was proposing love. Actually, I turned him down. He was furious and he said what he wanted all this time. He told me that he wanted his brother's property and even me; I was his brother's property too. He is married but he wanted to take his wife to my stand and become a polygamist, controlling my property and me. Truly, I said a big "No!"

Mrs Z. arrived in Sengezi with her husband in 1981. She became a widow in 1985, and her name was put on the permits. Her son from an earlier marriage lives with her and is building a house on her stand for his family. Mrs. Z explains: "My life is better than in communal areas. I want to tell you the truth, my dear … Imagine, if it was in communal areas, I would be chased away but now I call it my stand. If it was in communal areas, they will not allow my son whom I have with another man to build a house at their stand. But now, I do what I want."

While the dominant pattern in resettlement appears to be to allow widows to remain on the husband's stand, there are cases where an individual resettlement officer may disagree with this practice or let himself be persuaded by relatives to allow a more traditional course of action (Rukuni 1994; Chenaux-Repond 1993). In Sengezi, the resettlement officer stated that disputes over succession to resettlement plots were among the major conflicts he had to deal with. Relatives of the deceased often want to base succession on customary law of inheritance and have a brother of the deceased take over, but according to the resettlement officer, this is no longer considered appropriate and the Resettlement Office always refuses and awards the plot to the spouse. In rare cases, however, the Resettlement Office fails to enforce this policy. In one of the villages on the scheme, a male relative of a deceased permit holder arrived as a "caretaker" to the stand of the widow while she was still in mourning. The relative then refused to leave, even when the matter was reported to the Resettlement Office and the district administrator's office. The resettlement officer at the time of the study, who took up the position in 1994, inherited the problem. He wrote a letter of support for the widow, and the matter was reported to the police. Meanwhile, the widow had become homeless, unable to return to the stand because a son of the interfering relative had threatened her with an axe. The relative even claimed the free fertilizer designated as the widow's.

This ambiguity is partly rooted in the fact that while widows have tended to be allowed to succeed to the permits, they have no official written right to do this. This situation signals the incomplete nature of the state's commitment to this provision, in itself an instance of Cheater and Gaidzanwa's (1996) analysis of the Zimbabwean state as patriarchal. The incompleteness of the state's provision means that women are vulnerable to the decision of the resettlement officer, who may find in favour of relatives claiming their rights through customs still practised in communal areas. It may also occur that while a widow succeeds to the permit, property such as cattle, agricultural implements, and bank accounts are taken by the deceased's relatives. Hence, while she may retain access to land and a homestead, she may lose the means with which to farm productively (Chenaux-Repond 1996: 14). Here we see the WLSA's description of women living in the "shadow of the law" in action (Stewart et al. 2000). Although the state has taken a position in favour of women, women still have to negotiate for that benefit through their families and communities.

Deepening the tenuousness of these advantages for widows is the adoption of the Land Tenure Commission's (1994) recommendation to change the permit systems to long-term leases with an option to purchase after ten years. (The Land Tenure Commission is discussed in more detail at the end of this chapter.) With this shift to title deeds, the commission recommends the application of common law with regard to inheritance. Common law strengthens the rights of the surviving spouse and children vis-à-vis the husband's relatives (Stewart 1992). This may protect widows from the dominant experience in the small-scale commercial farming areas (formerly Native purchase areas), wherein the courts usually rule in favour of male heirs and reject pleas by widows to succeed to the title deeds of their deceased husbands. The courts use customary law to decide inheritance, as most deed holders die intestate and most marriages are unregistered African customary marriages. This was true in the mid-1970s when Cheater did her work in purchase areas, and it is still true today (Cheater 1981: 372; ZWRCN 1996: 18–19).

Women in resettlement do not see the application of Common Law as providing enough security in inheritance rights. Part of the problem is that inheritance laws do not deal directly with land. Thus, even though the Administration of Estates Bill, which was still in the printing stage at the time of this research, strengthens the rights of widows and children in regard to moveable property, the question of the inheritance of land rights remains open to dispute. Many women believe that the deed, permit, or lease should automatically go to the surviving spouse without contestation. This would be facilitated by the issuing of joint permits, leases, or title deeds (Chenaux-Repond 1996). Women's groups hope that the question of inheritance of land rights will be dealt with directly by the proposed land act being drafted at the time of this research. The act is intended to consolidate all legislation pertaining to land and is supported in theory by the former minister of lands and water development, who stated that there should be only one inheritance law that includes both land and property. This law, he said, must support a widow's right to stay on the land with her children.[3] The current climate of support for customary law by the courts, however, seems to run counter to the spirit of the act.

DIVORCED WOMEN

The prevailing situation for women who become widows on a resettlement scheme is clearly an improvement. Allocating permits to unmarried (divorced) women in their own right is also undoubtedly an advance in terms of women gaining land rights. As mentioned above, a very small proportion of divorced women with dependants were allocated resettlement stands across the country. In the Sengezi Resettlement, the stories of three divorced women who hold stands reveal both the advantages and limitations that primary land rights avail to poor women.

Mrs M. was married in 1950 and lived in Mozambique with her husband until 1973, when they divorced. Her husband had married his deceased brother's wife and no longer cared for her or her children:

My dear, life for me became difficult since he first made love to his brother's wife. She has strong love potions and I became nothing. Every day he came to my house with a new box of matches and he told me to light the match and find my way to my parents. He said maybe I am in the dark so I want light to find my way home ... He gave me my children only and I packed just a few clothes because it was a long way from Mozambique to Zimbabwe. I managed to carry my six lovely plates and a tray ... I walked a long way with my children, and then we boarded a bus to Mutare, then to our home area here in Wedza.

After eight years with her parents, Mrs M. applied for a stand and came to Sengezi in 1981. While she still lives in poverty, she has a place of her own and her children to help her.

Mrs C. was married in 1961 and divorced in 1971. She came to Sengezi alone. The divorce was bitter: "He burned my clothes and I just went to my parents with only one dress. He said he didn't want other men to love me wearing his dresses. I took my six children … My life is now better but I suffered the untold sufferings. I sold second-hand clothes and tomatoes, vegetables, and sometimes my body, but it was in 1974–78. From that time I became steady. Now I am fine."

The fascinating part of Mrs C.'s story is that all these years later her husband has come calling for reconciliation, and the reason is her land.

To my surprise he called me for reconciliation this year [1998], after the death of his [second] wife. I refused because I didn't know the cause of her death; maybe it's the killer disease [AIDS]. He is trying but [can give me] nothing I want because I have suffered already. I suffered paying school fees for my six children … He told me to forgive him and become his wife again. I don't think that will work. He is now about to go for his pension days and he doesn't have a house in the rural areas so he said he would come and stay with me. I asked him about his other six children [i.e., those of his second wife] – where are they going to live? And his answer was: I am their mother too. To be their mother now? What about that time? Why did he divorce me and live peacefully with his [new] wife?

Mrs C., clearly finds that as a land-rich, independent woman she is in an unusual position of strength.

Mrs P.'s story is somewhat different. She was married in 1979 and divorced in 1993. At that time she went home to her parents and then got a resettlement stand in her own name. She then reunited with her husband for two years, and they lived together at Sengezi. They divorced again in 1995. Since the stand is in her name, she was able to stay on this land and force him to return to his parents. However, he took everything else with him, including the children, furniture, chickens, cattle, and the harvest for that year. She lives in poverty, finding it difficult to get the inputs for farming. "My boyfriend is poor," she says.

These stories of divorced women with land outline how land entitlement protects women's interests, carving out a new mode of survival for women whose unmarried status often leads them to destitution. The stories also reveal, however, the limitations of land entitlement in alleviating divorced women's poverty. Two of the three women were left with their children to raise on their own; without the labour and at least occasional income of a husband, all three of these women find it difficult to advance economically.

The experience of divorce and the implications vis-à-vis a relationship to the land are very different for women who come to resettlement as married women. "Married woman" is the status of the majority of women in the site. In such cases, the norm has been to issue the resettlement permits in the name of the husband only (see chapter 3). As the district administrator of Wedza puts it, "Ministers do not want to change culture." Or, as the minister of lands and water development put it more specifically, the sharing of land rights between married people is a "private" or "domestic" affair. He gave this as a reason not to legislate for joint permits, leases, or ownership.[4] Readers will recall the discussion in chapter 2 of the seeming impossibility of married women having primary rights to land and President Mugabe's memorable comment: "If women want property, then they should not get married" (cited in Cheater and Gaidzanwa 1996: 200). This comment is a key example of the seeming intractability of the patriarchal nature of the state, again signalling the state's limitations as a force for women's advancement. In practical terms, this situation means that women who are divorced by their husbands on resettlement schemes are particularly vulnerable to losing their rights to land. All studies, including those in Sengezi, have found that a woman who is divorced by a male permit holder must leave the resettlement scheme. Since a wife's name does not appear on the permit, she has no official claim to the plot and usually has no choice but to return to her natal home. With two exceptions, all forty Sengezi respondents who were asked the question, both male and female, said that a divorced woman must leave the scheme and return to her home. This often means leaving her children, who in Shona customary norms belong to the husband. Of the two exceptions, one woman said that she would stay on the scheme with the children and her husband would go back to his home. The other woman said that her first choice would be that her husband build her another hut, as she did not want to leave her children; if he would not do this, she would have no choice but to leave.

As already introduced in chapter 3, inherent in marriage in the context of resettlement is a clearly gendered construction of property ownership. Much of the most valuable household property, such as agricultural implements, furniture, cattle, and the buildings on the home site, are seen as belonging to the husband. The wife is said to own the kitchen utensils, property she has worked for over and above her duties to her husband's land and domestic work, and any property given to her as a result of her status as a mother. This latter, known as *umai* property, is property a woman has obtained through a marriage or pregnancy of a daughter. For example, it is customary in some places for mothers to receive a suit of clothes from a new son-in-law, a head of cattle (*mombe youmai*), and possibly payments in cash, although these latter would always be very small compared to the cash paid as *lobola* (bride wealth, or marriage consideration), paid to the father of the bride. Upon divorce, a wife is entitled to take all such property with her. This includes any women's crops (discussed in chapter 3). In my case study, this pattern dominates: "the woman moves out and takes all her belongings, including the crops [harvest]; the man stays behind" (Male Farmer 3).

As became evident in discussions with the women's groups in the PRA workshops, fairly high rates of divorce prevail in the study site, serial monogamy apparently being preferred by men over polygyny. The story of Mr T. is illustrative. Mr T.'s uncle told us about the four wives his nephew had married and divorced in succession between 1980 and 1986. All four were chased back to their parents' homes, and none of them were given any crop yields. They only went with their clothes and their pots. In contrast, Mrs S. (according to the uncle of Mr S.), was forced to return to her natal home, but she was sent with all her belongings and many household goods:

Her husband hired a lorry and he gave her everything – property, chairs, tables, wardrobes, kitchen units and a bed. He gave her every crop in their granary. She was given the curtains, hoes and flowerpots ... When the lorry came and she was sure that he no longer loved her, she ran away and hid in her friend's house. The husband was serious; he first loaded the lorry with everything, and then after that he started looking from door to door. When he found her, she refused to go back home and get into the lorry. Then she was beaten and he tied both her legs and hands and threw her into the lorry. She went crying and we felt sorry for her.

While individual stories may vary in the type of property that goes with a divorced wife, the common thread is the loss of access to the homestead and the land. This reveals the precariousness of all married women's relationships to land in resettlement. With no automatic access to a resettlement stand of their own, women are just a divorce away from landlessness. Their vulnerability in this respect is explored further in chapter 7 through an investigation of husband-taming herbs.

CONCLUSION

The relationship of widows and divorcees in resettlement to agricultural land clearly reflects intersections of institutional forces, ideology, day-to-day labours and experiences, and the strategic agency of women working within the constraints of unequal power relations. Widows have been quick to take advantage of state support to challenge prevailing gender norms and take control of resettlement stands after their husbands' deaths. They do this in a context of contestation from their husbands' relatives and of somewhat ambiguous male support in the resettlement community at large. An interesting comparison can be made with the effect of titling land in Kenya starting in the late 1950s, a subject studied by Mackenzie (1990). Mackenzie argues that men creatively use customary law to challenge women's attempts to gain control of land from the patrilineal line. Since land is titled, statutory law applies and a widow can therefore inherit title to the land. She is challenged with customary law, however, if she attempts to pass the land to a daughter. The overall effect, Mackenzie argues, is the narrowing of women's access to and control of land. In a more general overview of women and land in Africa, Gray and Kevane (2001) note that, overall, women's access to land is declining. Although the reasons vary dramatically from place to place, a major factor is men's ability to negotiate new or strengthened rights in changed legal or economic contexts. While the process of securing women's access and entitlement to land is complex and not necessarily solvable through titling or other individualized tenure provisions (Razavi 2002), the important point here is that this effort is inseparable from prevailing gender relations and ideologies at the level of the household, the family, the community, and the state.

In the case of resettlement in Zimbabwe, the key institutional factor in the widows' success in improving their land entitlement is the authority of the state (however partial and compromised) to force a change in practice. Furthermore, the effects of this change are both practical and ideological. The state's support for widows affects what happens to them in a practical sense, which in turn helps to destabilize gender norms and ideology about what *should* happen to widows.

As the numbers of widows increase on resettlement schemes, their experiences of entitlement become a new norm that destabilizes gender ideology. As the main beneficiaries of this destabilization, women embrace the new norms wholeheartedly and become agents in enforcing them. Men lag behind somewhat, harkening back to tradition in some ways, but they nevertheless accept the new moral regime as it applies to widows. In general, women are quick to see advantages in state-backed moves away from custom.

Overall, the evidence given in chapters 3, 4, and 5 indicates that aspects of resettlement policy and process in the 1980s and 1990s created strategic opportunities for some women, especially widows, to improve their access and entitlement to arable land. Married women in resettlement schemes reported that their families' access to large arable fields in resettlement had improved their ability to grow crops over which they would have control, and a women's group in one of the study villages engaged in a successful cattle-fattening project. Through this, these women successfully appropriated cattle production from its social location as a male preserve. Local state officials considered resettlement women to be the main farmers of Sengezi, even though most of the men also resided in the area and worked on the fields. These dynamics clearly allowed the category of "women" to stretch in meaning and character. Women were clearly transforming their relationship to land in ways that improved their legitimacy as eligible subjects for land allocation, at least in the eyes of local state authorities.

Unfortunately, many of the changes documented here that are positive for women may be under threat in the contemporary context of fast-track land reform. These concerns are addressed more fully in chapter 8. However, at the time of this study, the mid-1990s, there were already extensive debates about land tenure and inheritance issues in regard to resettlement, debates that often tended to marginalize women's interests and thereby indicate key sites in women's struggle for land rights. These sites would endure up to and during the fast-track process.

The 1993 Land Tenure Commission (Rukuni 1994) was appointed by the president of Zimbabwe to investigate the major issues in all land categories in Zimbabwe and, through its recommendations, act as a central vehicle of land reform. Although it had no specific brief to examine gender issues (significant in itself!), the commission consulted women on some topics and reported on their perspectives in its report. Local feminist activists undertook their own extensive study on women's perspectives on land reform and submitted it to the commission (ZWRCN 1994). All of this occurred in a context wherein the Zimbabwean government had signed, in 1991, the United Nations Convention on the Elimination of All Forms of Discrimination against Women, Article 14 of which declares: "State parties shall take all appropriate measures to eliminate discrimination against women in rural areas, in order to ensure – on a basis of equality between men and women – equal treatment (of women) in land and agrarian reform as well as land settlement schemes."[5]

In its final recommendations, however, the commission almost entirely ignored women's views and interests. For example, it recommended changing the land tenure system from one involving permits to one involving long-term leases leading to title deeds. The government adopted these recommendations, although given the delay in the resettlement program, the implementation of new tenure arrangements was also delayed. The matter of inheritance law also remained unclear. While the commission recommended the application of common law to inheritance, elsewhere it recommended the extension of customary law in this regard in both resettlement and communal areas, a move that the government seems to be following with its new Traditional Leaders Act (see chapter 8).

In the mid-1990s, women's groups and farmers felt that the proposal for title deeds and the imposition of customary laws of inheritance would heighten women's insecurity in terms of their entitlement to resettlement land in two significant ways (Chenaux-Repond 1996). First of all, women farmers feared that a change from the permit system to long-term leases and title deeds would entrench male control of the land and do nothing to relieve women's insecurity.[6] If the husband's name stands alone on the lease or title deed, nothing changes for the wife. Only jointly issued permits, leases, or title deeds would increase women's land security in resettlement areas (Chenaux-Repond 1996: 24). This would help divorced women as well as those who remain married. Second, the advantages enjoyed by widows in the early resettlement program would be threatened by the application of customary law. Customary law, under which land rights are transferred to a deceased man's brother or eldest son rather than to the widow, would threaten the innovative resettlement policy of allowing widows to succeed to permits on the death of a husband, a policy that has clearly had profound material and social benefits for widows. The reversing of this policy represents one of the most profound potential losses to women in the current land reform process. It is hoped that the changes to inheritance law made in the 1990s that improve the right of widows to property will soon be expanded to include inheritance of rights to land.

The Land Tenure Commission's recommendations are informed in part by the paradigm of sustainable development, which privileges ecological sustainability while maintaining high productivity in land use. This discourse fits well with the increasingly tenuous link between land reform and social justice concerns, as documented in chapter 1, but the commission challenged this discourse by insisting that small-scale farmers both in resettlement and communal areas had been very productive in the post-independence period. Certainly, however, questions about gender justice in access to and control of resources, about inequality in the intra-household distribution of the benefits of resource use, and even about gendered divisions of labour have appeared to be beyond the interest of much of the sustainable development discourse.[7] Indeed, as discussed in chapter 2, the legal system and the state in Zimbabwe have apparently abandoned gender justice altogether. Increasingly, state and legal authorities have been making arguments against equality for women, pointing to African custom as a reason to return women to minority status legally and socially. These moves in the legal arena are strong signals indicating a reversal of the progressive stance on gender issues that marked the early post-independence period in Zimbabwe. The current contours of the struggle for women's land rights, which are still shaped largely by issues of inheritance, tenure type, and other legal provisions, are addressed in the concluding chapter. But first we dig deeper into the institutional and social dynamics that define and reproduce women's tenuous relationship to land.

6 Local Institutions, Land, and Environment

"People are not appeasing their ancestral spirits."

INTRODUCTION

The discussion thus far has focused on the effects of resettlement policies, processes, and agents on women's relationships to land, economic activities, and household form and dynamics. We have seen that women negotiate and claim advances in a dynamic context, wherein the powerful but incomplete reach of the state plays an important framing role. The other key forces shaping the space for women's negotiations are the practices of men, especially husbands and male relatives, within their families. The men in women's lives often utilize patriarchal and patrilineal gender relations of power, frequently drawing upon traditions such as marriage and inheritance customs to justify their opposition to changes and advances for women. The term "traditional" is discussed in detail below.

In this chapter, we see these dynamics again through further examination of the local institutional context. Both the local-level, state-sponsored institutions (Village Development Committees or VIDCOs) and emergent traditional beliefs and institutions influence evolving practices and values regarding women's relationships to land, political life, and place in the family. The incomplete reach of the state is seen in the failure of the VIDCO system to significantly promote women's political participation and leadership opportunities. On the other hand, the ways in which traditional practices and

institutions are deployed in this context underpin and express patriarchal and patrilineal control of land. These dynamics help to explain
the complexities of women's struggles for land entitlement, as well
as the tenuousness of women's relationship to land. Our investigation of tradition also looks at ecological elements of culture, especially
the particularity of the cosmological understanding of human/envi-
ronment relations. This underlines the importance of seeing women's
relationship to land from a more comprehensive perspective, going
beyond the mostly economic and social elements of agricultural production, household dynamics, and survival that have been the focus
thus far.

The insights of feminist political ecology are especially useful in
theorizing the local institutional context and gendered human/envi-
ronment relations. The importance of a micro-level focus on local institutions is strongly emphasized in the literature (Sachs 1997; Bruijn et
al. 1997; Rocheleau et al. 1996). In Sengezi, there are important differences in the ways that men and women relate to both state-sponsored
and traditional institutions. These differences marginalize women and
reinforce the secondary nature of their relationship to arable land and
other natural resources. Another key institutional issue highlighted by
feminist political ecologists is the way in which marriage tends to
mediate women's rights to natural resources (Fortmann and Nabane
1992; Nhira and Fortmann 1993). The evidence presented in earlier
chapters and added to here strongly supports this claim, illustrating
how the treatment of women by both state and community is powerfully shaped by perceptions, ideals, and practices of marriage. In this
mediation, women's relationships to land and natural resources are
consistently marked by asymmetrical entitlements shaped by gender
systems under which women have only secondary rights to resources
and men have primary rights (Thomas-Slayter, Wangari, and Rocheleau
1996: 291). There are multiple ways in which women's entitlements
are asymmetrical and secondary, as well as profoundly vulnerable, a
point pursued further in the next chapter.

Feminist political ecology also reads gender as a "meaning system"
that is produced not only through economic relations and cultural
and social institutions, but also through an ecologically based struggle (Rocheleau et al. 1996: 18). This environmental approach sees the
environment not just as a source of natural resources for human use
(e.g., as arable land is a source of crops), but as part of the total social
system shaping human life. Thus the environmental approach pushes

on the boundaries of materialist political economy approaches, which tend to follow Western social science in confining analysis to "the social" (assumed to be separate from the "natural" world). Indeed, this approach can be read as a return to Marx's dialectical view of "Man and Nature" and hence as a useful starting point from which to challenge human/nature dualist thinking. According to Marx, "Man" is seen as part of "Nature" but at the same time is driven to transform it and in the process is transformed by it (Salleh 1997: 71). One theorist reminds feminists to challenge the "conceptual gulf" in linking nature and "the social" (Salleh 1997: 183). Feminist political ecology takes up this call by interrogating the specificity of the cultural/social system of human/environment relations in different contexts in order to reveal further layers of gender relations and how these relate to broader social organization, process, and meaning systems.

LOCAL STATE-SPONSORED INSTITUTIONS

It has already been discussed that women in Sengezi have benefited from the "enlightened" attitude of the state representatives in the resettlement area, the resettlement officer and the Agritex extension worker. Both men supported the idea of women as farmers in their own right, the family ideal in resettlement areas of husbands and wives working together as full-time farmers, and the right of widows to maintain control of resettlement land. As mentioned in chapter 2, in the early 1980s, the state made numerous legal and institutional moves to promote greater gender equality; these changes flowed from the socialist ideology of the revolutionary struggle and the important roles that women played in the revolutionary war (Jacobs and Howard 1987). This early commitment to gender equality affected the formation of new local-level institutions. In 1984 President Mugabe created Village Development Committees as the new basic organizational unit for rural development (Higgins and Mazula 1993; Alexander 1994). VIDCOs were to be secular and democratic, a departure from the traditional local institutions, which are based on ancestral religion and lineage membership. It was easier to impose this new structure in the new resettlement areas than in the already established communal areas, not only because the settlements were new and therefore had no pre-existing leadership structure, but also because the settlers came from different original home areas and hence the patterns of local lineage leadership had been disrupted by their moves. Traditional leaders such as headmen did not go to resettlement. Readers will recall from chapter 2 that it was often the social misfits who were resettled, not the leaders and the well-established inhabitants of the communal areas.

At the village level, the village chairman is elected by democratic vote and can be deposed if his performance is unsatisfactory. The job of the chairman is to channel grievances or issues of dispute from the settlers to the resettlement officer and to take information given by the resettlement officer back to the settlers. The chairman is not part of the VIDCO, his duties being of a different nature. VIDCOS are meant to stimulate grassroots self-help development in the rural areas by developing local-level, ruling-party presence and machinery. Ideally, they are meant to decentralize the political structure and promote equity, empowerment, and economic development (Higgins and Mazula 1993). In practice, the VIDCO has often served to ensure centralized party control rather than to decentralize political power (Alexander 1994); this tendency was clearly in evidence in Sengezi in regard to the distribution of drought relief, for example. A VIDCO has six members (two members from each of three villages), one of whom is the VIDCO chairman. Six VIDCOS make up a ward, and a WARDCO is made up of a ward chairman, or "councillor," plus the VIDCO chairmen from the six VIDCOS. VIDCOS are meant to assist the village chairman in administrating the villages according to resettlement rules. Such duties include monitoring land and other natural resource use and management.

The post-revolutionary political commitment to gender equality meant that women are viewed as political actors who can and should be members of local and national political institutions (Jacobs and Howard 1987).[1] In the four core villages in my Sengezi study, local male and female key informants noted that there are some women on local committees under the VIDCO structure. However, as one prominent local male leader says, "women mostly don't have power in some of the activities done by men so they are active in their clubs but not strong in committees." While the new democratic institutions have expanded the possibilities for women's roles in local institutions, it appears that they have not been successful in promoting anything like equality in local governance. In a study of ten villages throughout Wedza District, Nabane and I found that women and men have very different relationships to local institutions and that they rank them very differently in terms of importance to their daily lives (Goebel and Nabane 1998). We had two Sengezi Resettlement villages in our sample. The men in one village placed great importance on institutions such as spirit mediums and traditional leaders, institutions that women did not mention at all. Women in that village ranked the Department of Social Welfare, which pays school and health fees for the needy, the District Development Fund, which provides boreholes, roads, and so on, and Agritex the highest. The men in the other resettlement village placed high importance on the VIDCO as the channel for all other institutions and on health workers. The women in the second village did not mention the VIDCO, but they too put health workers near the top of the list. Notably, women value highly those institutions that bring services to the village, not the institutions that are made up of local village membership. This should not be surprising, for even though many families have representatives on local committees and institutions, these representatives are nearly all men.

Women are somewhat removed, then, from the local state-sponsored institutions. This is another indication of how women are in "the shadow of" state policy and the law (Stewart et al. 2000). Village chairmen and VIDCOS have important roles in the management of arable land and other natural resources in the resettlement, such as woodlands, grazing areas, and riverine areas. Resources from all of these areas are crucial to women's daily survival activities (Goebel 1997). Women's political distance from the institutions responsible for the management of these key resources has the effect of continuing – albeit in somewhat modified form – the customary association of politics and leadership with men and, through this, reinforcing the secondary nature of women's relationship to the resettlement land.

TRADITIONAL INSTITUTIONS IN THE SENGEZI RESETTLEMENT

Tradition is implicated in important ways in the mix of contradictory and complex meanings for people's relationship to land. Appeals to and reinventions of tradition exist alongside different Christian sects, some of which forbid participation in traditional practices and ceremonies. In addition, modern practices and ideologies regarding land and resource use are imposed by state bodies and adopted by people to various degrees, along with differing levels of contradiction and/ or convergence with traditional or Christian meaning systems.

Shona traditional beliefs have strong implications for people's use and claims to land. They are also profoundly gendered through patrilocality and other aspects of gender relations, such as marriage systems and male and female roles and responsibilities. Before explicitly drawing out the gender implications of the deployment of tradition in the resettlement context, I outline key aspects of traditional religion as they relate to people's relationship to the land.

The word "traditional" is highly problematic, as it tends to imply a static system based in the past, one that would be in opposition to a modern, colonial, Western, or foreign system. Some authors prefer the term "indigenous," which embraces the system in active use by local people at a given time, a system likely to include elements of both tradition and modernity in complex interplay (Matowanyika 1991: 66–8). I use the word "traditional" in this chapter because it was the English translation of the Shona word that people in the study used (*Chivanhu chedu* – literally "things of our people," usually used as an oppositional term to *Chirungu* "things of the English or whites") when they categorized or explained different rules and practices in agriculture and the woodlands (see Guy Thompson 2002 on this linguistic pair). But I use "traditional" with the understanding that the traditions people describe are not timeless and unchanging, but represent current understanding and deployment of the concept of tradition by the people using the term.

Elsewhere (Goebel 1998) I have discussed how weakly formed traditional institutions in resettlement have contributed to a fairly strong resonance between local people's environmental analysis and the modern/conservationist position adhered to by the state and promoted through its agents in resettlement, the resettlement officer and the Agritex worker. This resonance or agreement is especially clear in people's analysis of such specific things as soil erosion in fields and along river banks, but less clear when the issue is a broader cosmological understanding of the human relationship to the land. This latter understanding is particularly evident in people's analyses of drought.

In communal areas, while the robustness of traditional institutions varies from place to place, the norm or ideal is for ceremonies to be conducted based on lineage history and membership. At the village level, a headman or kraalhead is named who has some blood connection to the overall leader of the area, the chief. The headman and the chief are responsible for traditional ceremonies that are for the protection of the whole community, such as rain making/calling ceremonies that are addressed to the ancestral spirits of the ruling lineage (known as "lion spirits" or *mhondoro*). These important spirits are thought to be able to intercede on the people's behalf with the remote high god, Mwari, who controls rain and other major environmental conditions, including soil fertility (Chavunduka 1997). They are believed to be the spirits of the original inhabitants of a given territory or province, and hence the religious system is sometimes seen to be made up of territorial cults (Schoffeleers 1979). Spirit mediums can be possessed by ancestral spirits and thus figure importantly in traditional custom. While mediums may or may not be members of the chiefly lineage of the area (Bourdillon 1987), they are often the ones to lay down traditional rules about resource use and management and proper behaviour in sacred places. These rules come from the lion spirits through the medium. According to traditional religion as it is commonly expressed across Shona country, wild fruit trees are not supposed to be cut, nor the fruit sold, and certain fruit trees may require special practices in order to be used. Sacred shrines, mountains, groves, wetlands, and pools all figure in Shona tradition as places that must be approached in certain ways, being homes or resting places for ancestral spirits. Tree cutting is often banned, along with disrespectful behaviour, in such places, linking ecological management with religious observance (Nhira and Fortmann, 1993).

Colonial governments were not specifically opposed to territorial cults, and except with regard to specific aspects of traditional religion such as ritual murder, they tended to leave these cults alone. In the nineteenth and twentieth centuries, Christian missionaries were disturbed by ancestral worship, polygyny, and beliefs in witchcraft and often preached against these practices and beliefs, but overall they favoured coexistence with, rather than eradication of, traditional beliefs. Prayers for rain were said in churches, and people were not prevented from flocking to traditional shrines in times of trouble (Schoffeleers 1979: 37–9).

The Shona people themselves tend to see the Shona religion and Christianity as compatible (Bourdillon 1987: 285–307; Chavunduka 1997). Besides community-wide ceremonies such as rainmaking, ancestral appeasement is largely a private family affair in Shona religion. A family's immediate ancestral spirits are thought to be intimately involved in the health and well-being of the living members of the family and require consultation and appeasement. If someone in the family falls seriously ill or faces other misfortunes (e.g., family disharmony, bad luck, or death), it is thought that the ancestors are displeased and require appeasement to restore their protection of the family (Bourdillon 1987; Chavunduka 1997). Many Shona people find that this private, family-based relationship with ancestors does not have to compete with a Christian relationship with God, which is largely individual, although strict Christians and followers of independent churches such as the Apostolic Faith may refuse to partake in family rituals and ask a traditionalist relative to perform his or her role (Bourdillon 1987). In addition, traditional religion in Shona societies includes the cult of the high god, Mwari, who is understood as distant and is rarely approached (Bhebe 1979; Bourdillon 1987). This pre-existent concept of a high god, whose nature is nebulous in Shona cosmology, is one of the reasons cited for the mostly harmonious past and present coexistence of the two sets of religious beliefs among Shona people. Indeed, about 40 per cent of the traditional healers registered with ZINATHA (Zimbabwe Traditional Healers Association) identify themselves as followers of both Christian and traditional religions (Chavunduka 1997: 43).

Christianity's influence on the transformation of traditional beliefs is clearly not a case of the dethroning of one system by another. Indeed, recent critical scholarship on religion in Africa (Comaroff and Comaroff 1991; Hefner 1993; Landau 1995) and in Zimbabwe in particular (Ranger 1993; Maxwell 1999) insists on both the historicizing of tradition and an understanding of Christianity in Africa that resists a dichotomization of tradition versus Christianity. Rejecting the view that Christianity was imposed from above on local African communities, new scholarship illuminates the "often unexpected process of inculturation from below: a process by which Africans appropriated the symbols, rituals and ideas of Christianity and made them their own" (Maxwell 1999: 4). I did not specifically investigate the nuances of local Christianity, but during my research it became very clear that people used Christianity and tradition as strongly dichotomous categories when making points about human/environment relations. This evidence does not contradict the literature on Christianity, but rather indicates an instance of the deployment of a certain set of social meanings in a particular context of social and institutional change. The strain on traditional religion that occurs as a result of weakly formed traditional institutions in resettlement appears to enhance the conflict between certain types of Christianity and traditional religion, with implications for people's cosmological understanding of human/land relations.

According to some scholars, far more important historically than Christianity in the weakening of the traditional systems were the alienation of land, the bureaucratization of the chiefs, and the imposition of rationalist conservation and farming practices (Schoffeleers 1979: 36).[2] All over Zimbabwe, traditional institutions and practices are in various states of strength and weakness; indeed, the country is marked by profound variation in local institutional dynamics (Goebel et al. 2000; Sithole 1997). Within Wedza District itself, Nabane and I found great variation among the eight villages we studied in Wedza Communal Area in terms of respect for local traditional leaders and adherence to traditional rules of resource use and management (Goebel and Nabane 1998). My intent here, then, is not to promote the concept of a dichotomy between communal areas as purely traditional and resettlement areas as modern or Christian; rather I point to how certain conditions peculiar to resettlement contribute to and further the dynamic and already profoundly transformed context of tradition in rural Zimbabwe. Also, I do not see tradition and modernity as distinguishable conditions in either time, space, or imagination, and prefer to use Sahlins's (1999) concept of "indigenizing modernities" as developed by Robins (2003) to capture the contemporary realities of "hybrid responses" to a history of colonial and post-colonial exogenous influences.

In resettlement, people come from many different villages and lineage groups. In the study site, while most people come from the district, they also come from a wide variety of home villages. In each of the four core study villages, most people come from villages not mentioned by other respondents. According to respondents, the main reason that people in the resettlement follow tradition less than in the communal areas is that they have originated from so many different villages.

In terms of land resource management, traditional leaders appear to have little power in the resettlement, although many people feel they should be involved. As mentioned earlier, people in Sengezi use the term "traditional" when they categorize or explain different rules and practices in agriculture and the woodlands. They speak of the chief in relation to respect for the sacred *chisi*, or the day(s) off ploughing, an important part of traditional culture. The chief may levy a fine (such as a goat) in cases where traditional rules are violated. It is said that spirit mediums and village elders ban the cutting of mobola plum trees (*muhacha*), considered to be sacred to the ancestors.[3] Traditional rules and institutions are particularly associated with herbs, small hills, and river areas. Herbs are used for traditional medicine, and small hills are used as burial sites and are the preferred places for ancestral spirits to reside. Many villagers mention that spirits inhabit river areas, especially pools.[4] People say wild fruit harvesting is regulated by traditional rules that forbid the harvesting or destruction of unripe fruit. Local people in the resettlement area list the traditional rules and institutions governing natural resources with great ease and consistency, and these rules and institutions are very similar to those found in communal areas (see Nhira and Fortmann 1993). However, in the Sengezi Resettlement, these institutions and rules fail to protect natural resources. For example, in some hill areas, so many trees have been cut down that graves are exposed. People are vague about sacred areas, although there is some indication that the ruling lineage of the nearby communal area is making some inroads in establishing sacred sites in the resettlement to be inhabited by their ancestors. The people in resettlement know very little about the original ancestral spirits of the area, the appeasement of whom forms a key aspect of traditional Shona religion.

The dominant view is that traditional leaders are not effective in creating traditional-rule adherence in the resettlement. People mention a variety of reasons for this, the most common being that people are stubborn – that is, they refuse because they do not feel like complying. Other reasons mentioned are that people are Christians, that they are modern, taking traditional as being old-fashioned, that the traditional leaders are lazy and never visit the resettlement, and that the VIDCOs have replaced their function. Thus, in the resettlement context, there is a space left by traditional leadership into which the VIDCO and the village chairman step. These bodies operate with a legitimacy deriving from a source different from traditional leadership, and they do not necessarily uphold traditional rules in land and resource management. Rather, their mandate is to enforce the state rules of the Natural Resources Board (NRB).[5] Although the two sets of rules and the attendant understandings of human/environment relations are different, there is essentially little conflict between the two sets of rules and institutions in Sengezi. In some rural areas, particularly in communal areas where the VIDCO and the traditional leader institutions coexist, there are conflicts over authority, but in other communal areas positions of authority in the systems overlap and the institutional structures coexist harmoniously (Goebel et al. 2000). In resettlement, it is generally not a case of conflict between the two institutional forces, but rather a case of an absence of traditional authority in a context of persistent traditional beliefs and values.

The lack of general institutional underpinnings for traditional religion may help to explain the overall lack of adherence to traditional rules specific to natural resource use. However, despite the apparently weak foundation for traditional practices regarding land and natural resources management and the prevalence of Christianity in the form of different denominations, people's broader cosmological and ontological beliefs about the relationship between the human world and the land are still profoundly shaped by Shona cultural heritage in ways that have important implications for women and for a gendered understanding of human/land relationships. This becomes apparent through consideration of people's analyses of drought and in some of the private family practices of ancestor appeasement.

ANALYSES OF DROUGHT

Central to Shona traditional belief is the power of ancestors of the ruling lineage to bring or withhold rain. These ancestors must therefore be appeased and special rainmaking and other supplication ceremonies performed, or drought may ensue.[6] As noted above, the link between ancestors and rain is part of a larger social system that includes other aspects of ecological management through religion. This system, variants of which are common to central Africa, link climatic and ecological processes to social cohesion and morality: "serious abuses in a community lead to ecological disaster which in turn threatens the life of the community" (Schoffeleers, 1979: 5). Traditional belief systems emphasize interconnectedness and respect for nature:

The Europeans think the human mission is to conquer nature. The African mission was the opposite. We did conquer nature, but in a small way which didn't injure it as we are doing now ... Most of our proverbs have to do with animals, with birds, and trees. After all, what do we talk about. We talk about our environment, and what experiences have we got without environment, without natural resources.[7]

Clearing the land for cultivation did not mean destroying forests. Huge trees had to be left alone. Herbs, shade, place of rest when a traveler is tired, all is provided by our vegetation. Every tree has a part to play in the life of human beings.[8]

In the Sengezi Resettlement, many people claim to be Christians. Moreover, the community-wide rainmaking ceremonies are rarely performed because of the settlement patterns and the absence of traditional leaders in the villages. Infrequently, representatives of the Mbire clan, members of the ruling Jena lineage in the next-door communal area, come to perform the rainmaking ceremony. The Mbire clan has also named some sacred areas. Nevertheless, the hold of traditional authority and practice is weak, for the reasons already mentioned. Despite this weakness, however, many people's analyses of drought reveal an enduring attachment to an ontology that sees the environment as inhabited by ancestral spirits who react to human behaviour. Here are some of the Sengezi settlers' explanations for recurrent drought: "I think people are not appeasing their ancestral spirits" (Woman Farmer 10); "People are no longer doing the rain ceremonies because most of them are Christians" (Woman Farmer 35); "People are now wicked, they are now too religious being Christians and abandoning their tradition" (Woman Farmer 5); and "People are now wicked; they do abortion and have dangerous medicine to become rich. God is now angry" (Female Farmer 8).

People in the study site overwhelmingly feel that although 1995/ 96 was a good rainy season, overall the occurrence of drought is becoming more frequent. Leading the reasons for this and for the causes of drought more generally is the people's failure to perform the appropriate traditional ceremonies. The two most frequently cited reasons given for this failure are, first, that people do not live according to lineages and, second, that people are more Christian than in communal areas. Many people identify themselves as Christians, and aspects of their religious practice sometimes cause social conflict – particularly the ban on participation in traditional ceremonies and the violation of *chisi* associated with Seventh Day Adventists and Apostolic Faith. However, there is no hard and fast line between

Christians and non-Christians, either in terms of belief in the ancestors or in the types of analyses given concerning the causes of drought.

As outlined above, traditional Shona culture links social and moral behaviour to climatic conditions. In the study sample (N = 60), while nearly half the sample said that the main cause of drought was the people's non-adherence to traditional rules, many people mentioned social crimes such as abortion, incest, murder, baby dumping, or witchcraft, or offered the more general observation that "God knows" or "God is angry." Christians and non-Christians alike link people's behaviours to the larger climatic forces that bring about drought, revealing a consistent philosophical stance regarding human/environment relations even if there are differences in their cosmological frameworks. The enduring traditional flavour evidenced in people's philosophical views on the relationship between human behaviour and drought indicates an ideological context still informed by traditional Shona religion despite the weak institutional basis for it and despite the competing ideologies of Christianity and Western conservationism.

The endurance of the ideological elements of territorial cults has gendered implications. Traditional Shona religion includes a division of labour among paternal and maternal ancestors. Paternal ancestors, particularly of the ruling lineage, are associated with environmental care and management, while maternal ancestors are seen as taking care of social and physical health and dealing with issues such as fertility and nurturing (Mutambirwa 1989). Thus, when people are concerned about environmental issues such as drought, soil fertility, and deforestation, the traditional religious implication is to turn to partilineal ancestors. In the study site, the distress people feel in the face of recurrent drought leads frequently to displeasure with the poor maintenance of the patrilineal order, which includes the ancestral spirits. Concern for this order is clearly a conservative force that is ideologically opposed to changes for women's roles and entitlements. The relevance of this dynamic for women and land is more obvious when the family-based rituals of ancestor appeasement are considered.

KUPIRA AND KUROVA GUVA

While Christian beliefs may keep some people away from community-wide rainmaking ceremonies (*mukwerera*) that are inconsistently held by the ruling lineage (the Mbire clan) in the area, the same cannot be said for the family-based supplication ceremonies. For example, most families in the resettlement area still perform *kupira* and *kurova guva.*

Kupira is usually done to appeal to the patrilineal spirits of the household in cases of illness, death, or disharmony in the family, but occasionally it is performed to appeal to maternal spirits (Bourdillon 1987: 52). Maternal spirits are seen as very influential in family health. Since a woman's natal family is viewed as having better access to her maternal spirits, appeals to these spirits are often done through that family (Bourdillon 1987: 32). It is the male head of the household who decides to hold the ceremony, and his wife is required to assist in the preparations. As one Sengezi man says, "I want to tell you this: when a woman is married, she is there to obey her husband's rules, so when I want to prepare my ceremonies she is there to do as I say."

People report that even Christian wives usually assist in these family-based ceremonies. In one woman's words, "As I said before: women are always behind men in Shona custom because that's our tradition. Some women are now following Christianity, but when the husband wants to brew beer for their family ceremony, they [the women] do it." A wife's family's ceremonies are held in her natal home, and she may be called to travel there to participate in the supplication of her own patrilineal ancestors.

Kurova guva, the other important ancestor practice mentioned above, involves the "bringing home" of the spirit of a person about a year after that person has died. This ceremony is usually performed only for the men in the family and normally in conjunction with an inheritance ceremony (Bourdillon 1987: 52).

Practices such as *kupira* and *kurova guva* support the patrilocal marriage system and patrilineal inheritance patterns and thereby maintain the primary connection of men with land and other natural resources. The persistence of these particular practices in resettlement helps to create a culturally defined ideological/moral climate – a sense of the "right" relationship to land – that clearly goes against women's claims to land in their own right, either as widows or divorcees. As discussed in chapter 5, most widows are successfully hijacking this pattern by "washing their sons' hands" at the *kurova gova* ceremony, thereby signalling their rejection of any possible suitors from her deceased husband's family and the naming of a son as the inheritor of herself and the resettlement stand. Widows are able to do this because of the support of the Resettlement Office. Here it is important to emphasize the strength of the cultural disapproval she is incurring as a result of her actions and the complexity with which gendered ritual, meaning, and human/environment relations are implicated in women's struggles for greater entitlement. Readers will recall that challenges to widows' succession to resettlement permits are among the most frequent and difficult problems facing the resettlement officer.

Overall, the resettlement site can be understood in an ontological context where the land remains populated by ancestors who demand that people follow certain rituals and practices that underline patriarchal and patrilineal control of land and other natural resources. The evidence presented here gives a glimpse of the cultural depth of people's opposition to the giving of land to women in their own right and, flowing from this, some of the limitations facing both women themselves and enlightened elements and agents in the state. Furthermore, there is little evidence that the new state-sponsored local institutions (e.g., VIDCOS) have provided women with a sustainable role in local political leadership. Women are active in their communities, in their clubs, and within income-generating groups, but these operate largely outside of, and are not connected to, the mainstream political organizations of local power and authority.

CONCLUSION

The implication of the theoretical arguments and accompanying evidence from Zimbabwe presented here vindicates the feminist political ecology approach that emphasizes the situatedness of human/environment relations and the importance of social institutions and gender relations and ideologies in understanding these relations. By focusing explicitly on human/environment relations, feminist political ecology also encourages us to go beyond social and economic considerations of women's relationships to land to appreciate broader cultural and ideological aspects. The approach offers much more than earlier approaches to women, environment, and development in Africa, which focused on the economic or livelihood aspects of environmental degradation and on women's roles as users, managers, and potential saviours of the environment.[9]

Feminist political ecology also escapes the limitations of ecofeminist approaches such as that developed by Vandana Shiva. Shiva views Western culture, colonialism, and capitalism as the basis of the global environmental crisis both in the North and the South (Shiva 1988; Shiva and Mies 1993). According to this approach, Western dualistic thinking posits "man" as separate from "nature" and hence as able to dominate and control it; it also underpins the dichotomous gender system that promotes male domination and control and equates women with nature. Shiva, then, stresses a relationship between patriarchy and environmental destruction, between the oppression of women and ecological disaster. Given the shared position of oppression of women and the earth, as well as women's association with life-giving and life-conserving work, women are conceived as having a "privileged epistemological approach to nature" (Littig 2001: 133) – a better understanding of both what is wrong with human/environment relations and how to promote positive change. Women's protests against environmental destruction and their knowledge about environmentally healthy practices are of key interest to those with an ecofeminist perspective.

Critics of ecofeminism cite cross-cultural evidence that suggests that a closer link – either physically or ideologically – between women and nature than between men and nature does not hold true across different contexts. One theorist points out that the connection of women and nature and a dominating ideology towards nature does not exist in Chinese culture (Li 1993). Leach's interesting study of the Mende in the Gola forest of Sierra Leone makes a similar point: the Mende associate certain aspects of the environment with men (such as bush) and others with women (such as fishing grounds) (Leach 1994). The Mende do not associate culture with men and nature with women; nor do they conceive of a culture/nature divide. Their relationship to the forest cannot be reduced to a mirror opposite of Western thinking (i.e., that there is no separation of people and nature). Rather, certain aspects of the forest are highly cultural (e.g., locations for communion with spirits) and associated with men; other places are wilder or, alternatively, more domesticated. Overall, Leach calls for a culturally and location-specific analysis of women and gender and the environment, as well as of "nature" itself:

Can all components and aspects of the environment be captured by a single concept such as "nature"? Rural African societies typically have complex ideas about the physical and non-physical attributes of different microenvironments, ecological processes and the resources obtainable from them. By failing to disaggregate "environment," ecofeminist formulations fail to ask whether different environmental categories are differently linked with ideas about gender. (Leach 1994: 33)

Leach also suggests that the presence of an ecologically friendly cosmology is no guarantee of sustainable practices in real life. Population pressure, social hierarchies, and economic necessity can lead to disjunctures between ideologies and practices. Finally, evidence from Colombia in a study of the Kogi people points out that a Mother-creator cosmology that appears female-positive – even feminist – in its valuing of female qualities of reproduction, care, and survival can coexist with practical relations of patriarchy and subordination of "real" women (Dodd 1997).[10]

My own evidence from Zimbabwe presented in this chapter supports these anti-essentialist critiques. On the whole, the research does not support a generalized view of women as closer to nature; indeed, women are distanced from the environment in significant ways through patrilineal culture and religion. Further, this distancing of women goes together with some elements of traditional Shona religion that indicate complex systems of ecological care and management. Hence, a positive cultural system in relation to environmental care goes together with what feminists would perceive as a problematic gender system. What is important, however, is that in the case of Zimbabwe, the religious and cosmological elements of human/environment relations and their effects on social institutions and norms are clearly central to understanding the ways in which gender is produced and, more specifically, the rigidities and challenges women face in negotiating more secure entitlements to agricultural land.

7 Gender Relations in Resettlement

"Men these days, they are a problem."

INTRODUCTION

As has been shown in earlier chapters, women as resettlement farmers in rural Zimbabwe are limited and disadvantaged by state and customary laws, practices, policies, and institutions. As a consequence, most women can gain access to arable land only through marriage and they face severe hardship if divorced. They have nevertheless been able to grasp new areas of opportunity. Examples of these opportunities include the relative land abundance in resettlement, which means they can grow more of their "women's crops"; the support of resettlement agents for their farming and other non-traditional income-generating activities, such as cattle rearing and irrigation farming; and the practice of allowing widows to gain control of resettlement land and permits after a husband's death. This study, then, has mapped out the major constraints within which women can negotiate change and grasp opportunities and the kinds of opposition these changes confront at various institutional, social, and cultural levels.

In this chapter, I shift the focus to the day-to-day dynamics of husbands and wives living together, the micro-relations of gender. As will be shown below, women are very active in their attempts to manage their husbands in the prevailing context of marital instability and devastating consequences for women of divorce. The evidence presented in this chapter suggests that women are engaged in complex, costly, and dangerous attempts to manage their husbands through the use of husband-taming herbs (*mupfuhwira*). We can read in these attempts expressions of women's agency and their own definition of their struggle. Women place great importance on this particular location of their struggle for survival – their marriage. Indeed, while gender-equitable legislation, equal opportunities for women as farmers, and the elimination of inequitable customary practices are clearly of crucial importance for women, in the current context, given the immediacy and brutality of the consequences of marital failure, it is the maintenance of their marriages that concerns women most. It is also at this very individual location of gender struggle that the implications of the broader structural conditions and constraints can most tellingly be read. More specifically, this chapter argues that the examination of the micro-relations of gender as expressed through the institution of husband-taming herbs reveals the all-important place of marriage in the lives of rural woman, the truly catastrophic state of marriage and gender relations in rural Zimbabwe, a clear picture of the gender relations underlying the HIV/AIDS crisis in rural Zimbabwe, the role of healers[1] in relation to marriage and gender relations, and some interesting dynamics of female friendships and female kin networks. In short, the study of husband-taming herbs provides an excellent vantage point from which to understand the lives of rural women in a resettlement context. This should not have surprised me, since from the very beginning of my fieldwork in Sengezi, women raised the issue of husband taming herbs.

MUPFUHWIRA: "LOVE POTION. 'MEDICINE' TO ATTRACT HUSBAND'S AFFECTION"[2]

Mupfuhwira, or husband-taming herbs, refer to a large number of herbal preparations and regimes that women may purchase from healers or be given by family or friends. The herbs are designed to control husbands' behaviour (especially infidelity) and promote love and harmony in marriage. *Mupfuhwira* must be distinguished from the various herbal and other preparations that reportedly most married women in Zimbabwe insert into their vaginas to decrease vaginal liquids and produce a "dry sex" experience for their husbands or boyfriends (Civic and Wilson 1996; Ruganga, Pitts, and McMaster 1992). Dry sex practices appear to have many parallels with husband-taming herbs, but *mupfuhwira* encompass more than dry sex herbs (I refer to dry sex regimes below). *Mupfuhwira* appear closer to the herbs for love and luck used by Tonga women in Zambia (discussed by Keller 1978).

Husband-taming herbs are mentioned frequently – and with great hilarity by women – and are greatly feared by men. Among the alleged effects of the herbs is that it enables a woman to "call" her husband from anywhere, keep him confined to the house, or control his behaviour in different ways. This attribute is especially useful to women whose husbands are given to adultery or excessive drinking. Apparently, a man drinking with his friends at the local bottle store will suddenly put down the beer pot and say, "I have to get home," without knowing why. The herbs deprive him of his autonomy and dignity, and are much more sinister (and sometimes more dangerous) than something that may be called a love potion. Chavunduka makes only brief mention of husband-taming herbs in his catalogue of different types of traditional medicines, placing them in with other good luck types of medicines (Chavunduka 1997: 78). He also mentions medicines that are available to husbands who suspect wives of infidelity. It is interesting that this type of medicine is placed under the category named as "instruments of law and order or for the preservation of morality" (Chavunduka 1997: 77). Keeping wives in order is a moral issue; keeping husbands in order is a question of luck!

We interviewed thirty people specifically about husband-taming herbs. Fifteen of these were healers who administer husband-taming herbs (eight women and seven men) in Sengezi and the Buhera Communal Area (the latter is next door to Wedza District). The female healers ranged in age from thirty-seven to sixty-one. The male healers ranged in age from fifty-six to seventy-nine. The interviews with the healers provided rich information on the perspectives and activities of healers, a privileged view of the cultural practice. The other fifteen people in our sample were all from Sengezi, and our interviews with them allowed us to get a general sense of the cultural currency and interpretative categories regarding the herbs. The ten women interviewed were between the ages of twenty-eight and sixty-one, while the men were between forty-seven and sixty-five. Five of the women identified themselves as users of husband-taming herbs, and all people interviewed claimed to have direct knowledge of cases where husbands had been tamed by herbs. While this sample of participants does not allow generalization to the population at large, the inclusion of the healers in the study as experts on the subject and the regularity with which the topic arose throughout my research allow the claim that the phenomenon is a significant social process in the study site.

Healers and ordinary folk alike estimate that nearly 80 per cent of all women use husband-taming herbs. At the time of the interviews, the healers had treated on average between two and three women each in the last week, with one male healer having treated ten women in the last week. The healers had treated on average more than five women in the last month and around twenty, on average, in the last year. Some healers had treated as many as fifty women in the last year. Overall, the female healers treat more clients than the male healers, a fact that will emerge as important below.

The healers listed the various preparations that they themselves prescribe. They also described how the herbs were prepared and used and what the effects of each were. In total, the healers mentioned over twenty different types of husband-taming preparations, most of them involving roots, the bark or leaves of trees, grasses, or other plants (a few involve gecko lizards and other wild animal parts). Each healer has between one and four different types that they use for different problems, and while the preparations of some of the healers may have similar elements to those of other healers, none of the healers offer exactly the same treatments. While the chemical properties of the plants used in the preparations have not been established,[3] symbolic values are strongly evident, as with many other traditional medicines (Bourdillon 1993). The concept of *tibatane* (sticking together, from the Shona verb *kubatana*) is strong. For example, a number of healers use preparations involving the bark taken from two different species of tree that are squeezed together as they grow, symbolizing fidelity and sexual attraction in marriage. *Nama*, or sticking grass, is another common ingredient, symbolizing the sticking together of husband and wife. Bathing and skin preparations are common, meant to make the wife appear beautiful in the husband's eyes and make her the only woman he would see with the eyes of love and desire. A preparation to avoid/prevent polygyny involves the use of two roundnuts in the same shell, symbolizing monogamy. To make a husband listen to his wife and do as she asks, there is a root that is put under the wife's tongue while kissing. Some of the preparations involve bodily fluids such as saliva, blood, menstrual blood, vaginal fluid, and semen, invoking the physical intimacy of marriage. Many of the regimens require adding preparations to food, tea, or beer, an activity that emphasizes women's power in the kitchen and the culturally accepted division of labour. This important theme is pursued below.

"PROBLEMS IN MARRIAGES MAKE WOMEN RUN UP AND DOWN FOR HERBS"

As these words, spoken by a woman who uses husband-taming herbs, suggest, women in Sengezi devote a great deal of time, energy, and money to husband-taming herbs. They do this because marriage as an institution is in crisis and the consequences for women are catastrophic. All except one of the people interviewed agreed that the use of husband-taming herbs is greater now than it was in the past. The reasons given for this increase will be dealt with below, but first the reasons for the use of the herbs are discussed.

One of the strong themes to emerge from the interviews with the wives is wife battery. Here are some of the women's voices:

I can't answer my child properly – after all I am nursing my wounds from their father's beatings.

I want to tell you the truth: my husband was sort of a killer in my life. I have four children with him, but most of the time he was beating me for no reason. One day he beat me right at the bus stop because I wanted to go back home to my parents. That's when someone felt sorry for me, a healer.

He sometimes beat me when I asked politely that I want some money to buy a new pot. I was advised by a friend to visit her usual healer after we discussed our problems ... I went to the healer.

The healers also mentioned domestic violence, but it was not one of the main concerns to emerge in their interviews.

The most frequently mentioned reason by both healers and ordinary folk for using the herbs was male infidelity. There was general agreement that married men's sexual and economic attachments to "girlfriends" and prostitutes are huge social problems. As one man said, "Some of the husbands are reckless and unfaithful." A female healer put it this way: "Men, they are a problem, they change [women] every minute." The reasons that male infidelity is defined as a crisis at this moment are complex. While male unfaithfulness is nothing new, the health risks of AIDS and other sexually transmitted diseases (STDS) pose serious dangers to married women; not surprisingly, STDS were one of the strong themes in the interviews. As one woman, a herb user, said, "I suffered from STDs several times and I doubt if I don't have AIDS because he was unfaithful … Long back the marriages were perfect because no matter if the men were unfaithful, there was no killer disease like AIDS." The healers, too, are very concerned about AIDS and see husband-taming herbs as a method to combat the disease. "The herbs avoid AIDS," said one female healer, while a male healer said, "They are bringing AIDS home, so to make him steady and faithful is the perfect thing; one woman is enough." HIV/AIDS is claiming a huge toll in Zimbabwe. According to estimates for the end of 2001, Zimbabwe's HIV/AIDS rate of infection was 33.7 per cent for people between the ages of fifteen and forty-nine, second only to Botswana at 38.8 per cent (UNAIDS 2002). As families bury their dead, agricultural productivity is decreasing, wages from former earners are lost, and the health care burden brought by the sick and dying is everywhere astronomical (Shiripinda 2000).

Although male infidelity may not be a new phenomenon, there is a perception that it has increased significantly. There is a common view that there are many women around who compete for the men. Married men, it is thought, are actively pursued by unmarried women and are therefore tempted into infidelity. As a female healer said, "So many girls to change from one to the other and the girls don't make their virginity precious, so a lot of things make wives running head over heels for husband-taming herbs." In addition, cultural and social changes have increased women's mobility and changed settlement patterns so that men and women come into more frequent contact. Another female healer stated: "Long back we lived far away from others, so to desire other women was a problem for men. Now everywhere there are women in beer halls, in roads and everywhere."

In resettlement areas, villages are arranged with houses close together so that people are in constant contact with their neighbours. In communal areas, despite colonial attempts to rationalize African settlement into concentrated lines, homesteads still tend to be scattered far apart from each other, although people congregate in shopping centres, beer halls, and so on. Reportedly, unmarried women, including prostitutes, use husband-taming herbs to steal the husbands of other women. As one woman said, "Even prostitutes are using these herbs, so it's good for a woman to start first before these prostitutes; women, we are competing for these men, so if you are lucky to be married, hold him tight, using anything to make love strong."

Women may be humiliated and hurt by their husbands' philandering with girlfriends, or they may be afraid of AIDS. But their main concern about relationships with girlfriends has to do with money. Men spend money on girlfriends, money that wives need to run the family: "Men, they can spend money with their girlfriends," said a female healer. Or as two married women who finally turned to herbs testified:

My husband was unfaithful and he didn't even support the family. I reported for maintenance last year, but I lost the case. I harvested my maize and we sold it; we sold our maize for $18,000 cash but I didn't use even a cent.

My husband was very unfaithful and he earns a lot of money. Before I used husband-taming herbs he was not giving me even a cent or buying me and the children new clothes.

Indeed, it is the women's need to control household budgeting that makes male infidelity so problematic. This need is mentioned by healers and ordinary people alike. As one man said, "If the husband uses the money on beer, women say that's money wasted. They want to control every cent: then poverty is the main thing." Or as two female healers put it, "Yes, now they are using [husband-taming herbs] more because of money and some they don't want their husbands to marry other wives. They don't want him to use a single cent. That's why they want to control [him]"; and "Now they are using [husband-taming herbs] more because of money and women think that they are better planners than men. Women think that they know how to use money." And when stories of success with husband-taming herbs are told, harmonious family budgeting is a key theme. As one man recounted, "I know a woman whose husband was very argumentative in the house and he didn't want his wife to use even a cent without his knowledge. The wife was given herbs by her aunt and the husband actually changed; he is now a quiet man and sharing his money with his wife in harmony." The issue of control will be explored further below.

Girlfriends pose an immediate threat to the family budget, but even more threatening is that girlfriends can lead to the marrying of other wives or, even worse, divorce. As one woman said, "When my husband brought his new wife, he made me pack my things and go after beating me." Or as another woman stated, "Men do painful things sometimes. They just take a wife, and after a year he becomes fed up and leaves her; then goes to another one. See maintenance cases, they are a lot but all of them who are dumped are women who wanted marriage. To be married after you are divorced is a hard thing in our society. You lose your dignity. It's better to get hold where you are by any means because a loser is a loser. It's now survival of the fittest."

As discussed in earlier chapters, divorce leaves women destitute. They lose their rights to children, homestead, land, woodlands, and a husband's income. Divorced women are social and economic outcasts. When women fight to avoid divorce, they are fighting for their lives.

The healers mentioned divorce over and over again. They feel that divorce is out of control and a major threat to the health of the society. Preventing divorce is their major goal in prescribing husband-taming herbs. Here are two views from the male healers: "We n'angas, we don't want divorce. We think we are building up the nation"; and "People are now using taming herbs more than before because if women don't use, they will be divorced ... I encourage them to use if they find good herbs for the sake of their children and dignity in society." While female healers share this concern for the overall health and dignity of society, they also express greater affinity for women's plight than do the male healers. The female healers, often wives themselves, express compassion through their shared position with the women they help. Therefore, while the male healers' concern with divorce is ultimately conservative, the female healers' concern often includes a radical element that supports female empowerment. One female healer stated, for example, "Women, they do it for love because they don't want to be divorced. Again, our husbands take us as toys, and I can say as someone who doesn't know, but it takes two people to make a good family; that's why I do that or help them to fight for their own rights." One female healer even condoned female infidelity, which a wife can hide from her husband through the "blinding" effects of husband-taming herbs. The healer cited women's devotion to family and her right to sexual satisfaction as justifications for this: "Let's say the wife is unfaithful: to me, I don't see any problem because she brings home what she worked for. And there are reasons which make that wife unfaithful. So I can say that if the husband has been told by someone [about the infidelity], let him not listen [through being given husband-taming herbs] so long as there is sugar and help from boyfriends and sometimes satisfaction for the wife."

This brings the discussion back to the issue of control. There is nearly universal agreement that male infidelity must be controlled in order to avoid AIDS and to ensure the economic survival of the family. But there is a distinct gender difference among healers regarding how much control is too much for women to wield. Male healers express disapproval of wives who seek what they see as too much control: for example, "Most of them, they come to me asking for herbs but they want herbs of controlling, not of living together nicely. Women they want to control"; and "Problems, they are there, but women also want to control too much. Some they want herbs to do all the work: they think they have to tame, not to know what their husband wants."

Male healers and ordinary men worry about women being out of male control, particularly in regard to female sexuality. As one healer said, "I treated eight women last month, but I am now ashamed because some are married women who wanted to tame their boyfriends. They have boyfriends while their husbands are away for work and they want to control the husbands' money also."

This story, told by a forty-seven-year-old man, expresses concern over women's mobility:

I know this man in our village, Mr ——, he was tamed. He was a man of his word, he controls and disciplines his family. The wife wanted to go to South Africa and buy and resell like other women who do it. He first denied her, and sure he had his reasons because a lot of these women are dying from AIDS. She kept quiet and she is a healer herself. Then she mixed her things and now the husband is useless – a "yes man." She is doing whatever she wants. She is now giving other people those evil herbs – imagine!

Another man speaks about how some men watch their wives' every move to try and prevent them from getting husband-taming herbs: "They [men] sometimes watch every movement of the wife; keep her from her friends or from talking to other people."

Clearly, there is a battle raging.

HEALERS' ANALYSIS: "WE PARENTS, WE CAN'T DO ANYTHING"

Both male and female healers identify economic and cultural issues at the root of the marriage crisis. Money is mentioned constantly as a cause of marital tension. The ongoing economic crisis, especially bad since the early 1990s with the implementation of ESAP (see chapter 1), has seen real incomes fall at the same time that subsidies on basic necessities and social services such as health and education have been reduced or removed. Rural society is a cash-dependent society. Money is needed for daily necessities such as cooking oil, soap, and candles, as well as for education and health care. Understandably, women are desperate for the only real route to money – marriage.

Money is also identified as a reason for the weakness of marriage as an institution. Healers point out that men can pay their own *lobola* (marriage consideration) from their cash earnings in wage work and thereby circumvent the need for parental help and approval in marriage. Without the son's dependency on the extended family, the family has no say in how the son behaves. One male healer explained: "We parents, we can't do anything because our sons they are now suing money themselves. He can just tell me that he has another wife and tomorrow another because he paid *lobola* alone using his own cash. We don't have a say when he divorces because I didn't help him; even polygamy is not the same as long back because now they first divorce then marry another one but long back the first wife was respected and stayed for the children." With the loss of the extended family's influence and what help such influence may have afforded wives in times of errant male behaviour, daughters-in-law have taken the matter of husband control into their own hands. A female healer stated, "Long back parents paid *lobola* and they had the right to stop divorce and daughters-in-law respected their in-laws; but these days they now rely on taming herbs for the husband to understand them. That's the only way they find respect – if they tame their husbands."

Changes in the dynamics of the extended family are also reflected in the predominant way that husband-taming herbs are used. Healers discussed how, in the past, husband-taming herbs were used like other traditional healing methods – in consultation with the extended family and the ancestors. A daughter-in-law could approach her husband's parents if her husband was behaving improperly or abusively. A traditional healer could be consulted to find out what was causing the bad behaviour and which herbs should be administered accordingly. One of the male healers interviewed still insists on this way of using husband-taming herbs:

I need the parents because they know the totem and all the channels of that generation and they tell their daughter-in-law what to say when using because most of the time it's something caused by the ancestors for a child to behave in a strange way. They tell her to say, "I beg from the young uncle or aunt, tell to the oldest of those who are dead" so that they can help their son to behave normally and lead his own family. In our culture everything is from the ancestors, so if a wife uses alone maybe it doesn't work. The totem is our guideline [for] we healers, so as to know which kind of herb to use.

But this healer finds himself with few clients: "They don't want my kind of herb because I always ask her to bring the husband's parents or relatives: they want to do everything privately."

While the interviews do suggest that most women use the herbs privately, family does emerge as a theme. Most of the healers interviewed mentioned that they administer herbs to their own family members, as well as to strangers. A female healer had recently given herbs to her four sisters-in-law because, as she said, "I wanted my brothers to stick to their wives because they will die of AIDS." A male healer said that he had treated about twenty women in the last year, attributing this number in part to the fact that "I gave [herbs to] my daughters." And, as shall emerge in the next section, the difficulty in getting good husband-taming herbs from a trustworthy healer places women who have the knowledge "in the family" in the best position.

WOMEN'S NETWORKS: "WOMEN, WE ADVISE EACH OTHER"

Despite the apparent prevalence of the use of husband-taming herbs, getting access to herbs that work can be difficult. Most women do not follow the "official" route of consulting parents-in-law, preferring to pursue informal knowledge networks. A woman's natal family can be an important, and perhaps the most reliable, resource, but friends seem to be the most common source of information about good healers. Here are excerpts on this subject from our interviews with rural women:

It is difficult to find the right thing and some other times people are afraid to be given poison to kill their husband, so through love and desperation a woman can succeed but after a hard time.

It's easy if you come from the family who knows all about it. It is difficult to us who don't know and me I don't trust.

Women find these herbs through discussion with friends because herbs and how to use herbs are ideas and advice from friends. So this depends on your friends.

It's easy to get herbs because we feel sorry for each other and we help each other.

It's not easy but we are getting them through thick and thin ... I am preparing to go to Mutoko, because another woman told me about another healer in Mutoko; the woman told me when we are at a conference at UZ [University of Zimbabwe] for the Women's Action Group [WAG].[4]

Men seem to be aware of these networks. The following remarks of one man were echoed by all the men we talked to: "It is sometimes difficult [for women to get husband-taming herbs] due to privacy, but they have sweet tongues to persuade those who know. No one will move around saying he or she knows, so they know through their women's gossiping."

Not only can it be difficult for a woman to find out where to go for the herbs, but she also appears to run a high risk of being given bad or even dangerous herbs. This may be because the "friend" who provides them is actually a jealous enemy, but more often it is because the healer himself or herself is jealous, greedy, or wicked and deliberately does harm or sells useless herbs. Here are some of the women's worries:

I know a story of another woman who had been beaten all the time and she told her friends and the friends gave her some herbs. She was told not to eat them but to give [to] him alone. She did so and the husband died. That is why I told you that sometimes you will be unlucky and find the jealous and witches. It's not easy to find the right type, but women, due to suffering and love for their marriages, they sometimes trust their friends.

Some other people they are jealous and have difficult kinds of herbs. Due to stories which I heard since long back, I was afraid of using these herbs. I can say I am lucky because my healer showed me the plants and how to do it so no problem. I shall tell my friends too.

We are so private in many things, so it is not easy to approach someone. I am lucky because my friend went with me to the healer herself. Again, women, we don't like the progress of other women. That jealousy causes women not to help each other properly, even women healers.

It is very difficult to find good herbs because sometimes the healers just want money, not to help people.

If they find the perfect thing and the correct herbs, the marriage will be fine and perfect; but if they lied to her and gave her the wrong herbs, that's when she will suffer untold sufferings.

Even one of the healers (a fifty-six-year-old man) stated that healers are not necessarily trustworthy and are sometimes dangerous, even murderous: "I want to tell you the truth: these *n'angas* have their *tokoloshi*[5] and some of these feed on human blood. So if a woman asks for taming herbs she will be given herbs to kill so that this *tokoloshi* has blood to feed on. They kill also for their rituals."

The activities described by this healer sound more like witchcraft than traditional healing. Witchcraft involves the use of herbs and spells for evil purposes, such as to give an enemy bad luck, illness, possession, or even death. In the broader society, accusations of witchcraft have reached alarming levels.[6] According to ZINATHA's analysis, as expressed by its head, Dr Chavunduka, economic hardship and social disintegration encourage people to look for scapegoats. Hence, people accuse neighbours of witchcraft, often taking matters into their own hands and burning the "witch's" house. On the other hand, people turn to witches to help them advance their own interests. As Chavunduka said, "There are witches in every stratum of society … and it is not only the ignorant who are bewitched. Even Government ministers are affected."[7]

As with *n'angas* and other healers, there is a distinction between witches, who are assisted by a malevolent spirit and often inherit their powers, and what Bourdillon labels sorcerers, who have an understanding of herbs and can prepare poisons that can be administered to enemies (Bourdillon 1987: chap. 7).[8] Bourdillon also points out that the powers of *n'angas* and witches are similar, the distinction being that the one uses their powers for social good and healing and the other for evil. This distinction is important because it helps rescue traditional healing from a colonial past that lumped it together with witchcraft. (Recently, ZINATHA [Zimbabwe's National Traditional Healers Association] proposed changes to the archaic Witchcraft Suppression Act [of 1899] in order to exclude from the definition of witchcraft genuine traditional healers and to help deter the practice and false accusations of witchcraft.)[9] The similarities between *n'angas* and witches are important for reasons more closely linked with the concerns of this chapter. Some traditional healers are known to use their powers and knowledge for evil and are said to be practising witchcraft in such cases. More subtly, some *n'angas* find it necessary to use medicines that cause harm, but for a good cause: "Even a right-minded healer may have 'medicines' which can cause personal harm in legitimate circumstances; he may have and sell, for example, charms against theft, which are supposed to cause the thief's abdomen to swell, and 'medicines' against adultery, with which a man can make his wife's lover severely ill" (Bourdillon 1987: 180–1).

The presence of people with such supernatural powers – both healers and witches – can produce a profound sense of mistrust and anxiety in a community. In the study site, there is a general atmosphere of suspicion among resettlement villagers. In my larger project (Goebel 1997), I found that many people in the Sengezi Resettlement are commonly thought to be involved in witchcraft, this being one of the reasons they were chosen for resettlement by their headmen in communal areas. Furthermore, Shona culture understands sickness and death as never accidental. A reason must always be found, whether witchcraft, an angry ancestor, or a malevolent spirit (e.g., *ngozi*, which are spirits of childless people, people murdered, or people for whom proper burial or other ceremonies following death have not been performed). A wife may be accused of being bewitched if a baby or young child dies. Parents of a son married to such a wife often pressure their son to divorce her so as to rid the family of the bewitching influences.[10] If a husband dies, his wife may be suspected of using taming herbs or even witchcraft or sorcery. This layer of potential danger involving the supernatural must be added to the analysis of the cultural meaning of husband-taming herbs. I pursue this and also give consideration to other risks in the following section.

"I CAN SAY IT'S GOOD ... AS LONG AS SHE DOESN'T KILL ME"

Husband-taming herbs can be very dangerous. Danger may lie in the physical effects of the herbs, in the possibility that a healer is untrustworthy, in the temporary effects of many of the herbs, in angering the man's ancestral spirits, in raising the suspicion or anger of the husband, which can lead to worse behaviour or divorce, or in the disapproval of the man's friends and relatives, who may notice a change in his behaviour.

The healers claim that most of their regimens do not cause harm, even if misused (which happens quite frequently). But some of the preparations can lead to serious harm if improperly applied. A female healer describes one of the dangerous types:

I have one kind of herb which is not all that good when it is used improperly. It is the *mushanje* roots and sperm. If she misuses the herbs, the penis will disappear with all the testicles. Everything will go inside, no penis plain, and the husband will become very fat that same day. I gave a woman that type and she misused it and what I told you happened to her husband. I was called, then I treated him. He became normal but she was divorced straight away. If the treatment came later than 24 hours, he would have died.

Another dangerous outcome of misuse mentioned by a number of healers and ordinary folk is that the husband might become "sleepy" or "useless." Sometimes this effect is so severe that the husband may quit his job. Here are the comments of two of the healers: "If she puts too much the husband will sleep most of the time. He will become useless"; and "If she keeps on giving the herbs to him he will become a fool, not knowing what he is doing." Ordinary folk, men and women, tell much the same story: "Some, they leave jobs because they are now like zombies"; or "If she gives him too much, that is when he will be useless, sleeping ..." One interviewee told this story:

I know a certain woman who found herbs to tame her husband. I don't know where she got them but the husband was not a problem at all, he just wanted everything to be smart. What happened is that after using the herbs, the husband refused to go to work and he always wanted to see his wife every time. He refused to go to work and as you know that everything is for money these days, she suffered a lot and the parents wanted their son to be cured. She had nothing to do ... the healer doesn't know the cure. She has to stay like that. See how evil it was? She has poverty even now but the husband loves her and she has to find a boyfriend who can support the family but the husband, no matter being told, he doesn't accept it [as the truth].

Perhaps the more sinister risks are those associated with being given bad herbs. Except for the one healer quoted above regarding the *tokoloshi*, the healers we interviewed did not admit to purposefully giving women bad herbs. But the men and women we interviewed spoke a lot about this danger:

But some, if they are unlucky, that is when the husband dies or becomes worse in his behaviour. Women's intentions were not on killing their husbands but are for love. The suppliers of these herbs are the ones who made the mistakes.

They are dangerous and a lot of men are dying because of these things. Imagine if there were good herbs, why even daughters and sons of healers, they are being divorced and sons don't get jobs. Truly, they are lying; the marriage is some other times destroyed by these herbs.

And if a man dies – whether from bad herbs, AIDS, or other illnesses – the existence of husband-taming herbs produces a cultural category under which the wife is brought under suspicion.

The death of the husband is obviously a serious risk of the herbs, but there are others that have terrible consequences for women, consequences such as divorce and worse behaviour on the part of the husband. In the case cited above about the treatment that caused the husband's penis to disappear, the husband divorced his wife. A number of the men and women interviewed mentioned that a woman may be divorced if the husband suspects she is using husband-taming herbs or if she uses them improperly. The risk of inducing worse behaviour is mentioned frequently: for example, "Others [men] become rude" and "He reacts and becomes harsh."

WHY DO IT?
"MY HUSBAND IS NOW A CHANGED MAN"

Why are women willing to face all the risks and dangers, not to mention the expense ("I paid a lot of money for this type … I grow vegetables for this purpose and sell"), of using husband-taming herbs? As shown throughout this chapter, women have everything to lose but they are desperate enough to use the herbs regardless. Perhaps it is this desperation that makes the stories of success so compelling, so wholeheartedly believed in, so very promising. Ordinary women and men, as well as healers, speak movingly about cases of changed male behaviour. Here are some of their tales:

WOMEN:
She went to another healer and she was given some herbs. Truly now, they are going together fishing and he is always with his wife every time. That's

why I said if someone is lucky to get the right type, everything will be perfect.

I gave him [taming herbs] in January this year and he is coming home, not sleeping outside as he used to do. He is bringing his pay. I told you, my dear, of the purpose. He was very very unfaithful – that is why I am using all kinds of herbs.

This caused no bad effects, but best, my dear: we are now darlings. I did it because he was very very troublesome.

MEN:
He came that same day to his in-laws. When he came face to face with his wife, that's when he said he thinks about her every time. That's why he came. She cooked some of the herbs in his food. From that time they became lovers till now. Imagine! After two years divorced and now she is controlling: no beatings, now perfect.

The wife was given herbs by her aunt and the husband actually changed; he is now a quiet man and sharing his money with his wife in harmony.

HEALERS:
The relationship will be fine and they understand each other.

Everything will be perfect; the love in marriage becomes stronger and the husband becomes very faithful.

They become lovers and faithful partners.

A further attraction of the herbs is the reported ignorance of the tamed husband about his state. Friends and family may suggest to him that he has been tamed, but he does not accept this. He cannot be dissuaded from his attraction to and trust in his wife.

More broadly, the use of husband-taming herbs fits within a cultural framework of marriage that requires secret maintenance work by wives. For example, the practice of placing drying herbs and other drying agents in the vagina to promote male pleasure through so-called dry sex is thought to be widespread in both urban and rural areas (Civic and Wilson 1996; Runganga, Pitts, and McMaster 1989; Kaler 2000). In the small but interesting study by Runganga, Pitts, and McMaster, Zimbabwean women reported that they almost always used drying herbs before sexual intercourse with husbands, and most claimed that their husbands did not know about it. The women found out about these drying practices either through traditional female networks, such as their aunts or grandmothers, or through the more modern networks of female friends. Women use these drying agents to increase the sexual pleasure of the husband and thereby keep him faithful (Runganga, Pitts, and McMaster 1989). Secrecy was also important in Keller's study of women's use of husband-controlling herbs in Zambia, as was wives' profound sense of vulnerability in a context of rampant male promiscuity and economic instability (Keller 1978).

CONCLUSION

One of the unexpected themes to emerge from our interviews was male vulnerability. The woman controls the kitchen, and it is this control that gives her the opportunity to administer husband-taming herbs. As one woman put it, "Men can't do anything to avoid [being tamed] because if he cooks, that's when people think that he was tamed or people say he is greedy, he wants to eat more meat. Our tradition is that women are supposed to be in the kitchen every time." And as several of the men said,

The trust I give to my wife is the one which kills me. One thing is that, traditionally, our wives have to cook. If my friend saw me cook that's when they say I am greedy and I am tamed, so [there's] nothing to do.

Men, we can't do anything because I marry her to wash and cook for me, so my life is in her hands. That's why if a husband died, the wife will be blamed all the time.

Nothing to do because if the husband cooks or does anything in the kitchen, that's when people think that you are tamed. If you marry, there is nothing you can do.

It is here that we see women's agency. Their control in the kitchen gives them a space to exercise what little power they can in their attempt to stay married. Women's agency is also seen in their manipulation of family-based traditional practices in ways that they perceive serves their interests better. But this agency is profoundly circumvented by women's ultimate vulnerability to male rejection and by the likelihood that family and society at large will blame them for any serious mishaps that may befall their husbands. The desperate position in which these dynamics leave women cries out for attention and redress. When a marriage fails, it is clearly the society's rules and customs, such as the lack of women's primary rights to land and the nature of the institution of marriage, that leave women destitute. However, in day-to-day life, it is the relationship with a husband that counts most – in all its physical, sexual, emotional, and negotiated complexity. As the women say, "Men these days, they are a problem."

Discourses around HIV/AIDS should attend to the complexities revealed here regarding sexuality. There is clearly a problem involving male power and promiscuity, but there can be a problem, too, in women's struggles to find and keep a man. Women's economic insecurity has a sexual expression that must be incorporated in the understanding of the role of gender relations in the HIV/AIDS crisis. The gendered cultural meaning systems and institutions related to marriage maintenance and interpretations of death also need to be considered in HIV/AIDS discourses. In helping women keep their marriages monogamous, harmonious, and long-lasting, healers clearly may promote behaviour change that assists the fight against the pandemic. However, mapping a way forward must take account of how secrecy, suspicion, and the supernatural figure in the way people manage marriage and analyse death. Overall, the explanatory richness of the investigation of husband-taming herbs points to the importance of locating analysis in local social categories, practices, and meanings.

8 Conclusions

The initial resettlement program in Zimbabwe brought with it new institutions and new types of state involvement in agricultural production, family dynamics, and gender ideology. The resettlement process also triggered intense cultural negotiations regarding people's relationships to land and natural resources, with important gender dimensions.

This phase of Zimbabwe's land reform process has had contradictory effects for women. In the case study of the Sengezi Resettlement presented in this book, these contradictions reveal important contours in women's struggle for land rights and the ways in which gender is created through the social relations of arable land. Aspects of resettlement policy and process created strategic opportunities for some women, especially widows, to improve their access to arable land. Married women reported that their families' access to large arable fields in resettlement improved their ability to grow crops that they could control. However, resettlement policy also maintained the customary approach to land, which prevents married women from gaining access to land in their own right. This structural position has made divorce a disaster for women in resettlement, and this is all the more problematic because marriages are highly unstable.

The tenuousness of women's entitlement to land must also be understood through the lens of culture, particularly through the ways in which tradition has been deployed in the resettlement context.

Although the traditional institutions are weakly formed in resettlement villages, aspects of traditional culture – for example, family ancestor appeasement and bringing home the dead – are commonly practised. These practices enact and express a cosmology that understands the environment as populated by and under the care of ancestral spirits. As Kesby has pointed out, the relations between land and tradition are also profoundly concerned with the construction and reconstruction of masculinity (Kesby 1999). This form of masculinity requires that women be distanced from the land as "outsiders" in patrilocal settlement, just as it requires that they be distanced from their children through the constructing of children as belonging to the patrilineage. Some geographical areas, or spaces, contribute to the destabilization of the status quo of gender relations through the disruption of the links between land and masculinity. Examples of such spaces are resettlement areas and, in colonial as well as postcolonial times, urban areas (Barnes 1999; Schmidt 1992b), mines, and commercial farms (Rutherford 2001b). While these spaces thus offer new opportunities for women to challenge tradition, they are also spaces where men work hard to use tradition to recapture patriarchal control – a dynamic that is grimly evident in urban areas in the escalating rates of rape and domestic violence (Osirim 2003).[1] The identification of homeless men, or grown-up "street kids" (arguably the most emasculated and marginalized of male subjects in contemporary Zimbabwe), as figuring largely in these urban rapes suggests as motivation an attempt to recapture masculine identity through the domination of women, this in a setting where the traditional means of achieving a masculine identity have vanished and modern means (such as obtaining waged employment) are unavailable. Osirim makes a similar point in relation to the horrifying levels of domestic violence in urban areas, particularly in low-income households. She points out that in the 1990s poor and low-income urban men found it increasingly difficult to achieve accepted masculine identities by providing income and protection for their families: "Under these conditions, men are increasingly taking out their frustrations on their partners. There is a strong belief throughout much of sub-Saharan Africa that men should have total authority in the home, and many men feel it is acceptable to hit women" (Osirim 2003).

The promotion of women's rights to land cannot be seen as simply a political project of the state (e.g., a question of resettlement policy and laws); rather it must be seen as a profound challenge to a living cultural tradition that understands land as a key element of hege-monic masculinity and patriarchy. The difficulties facing women who challenge prevailing gender norms will clearly deepen with the new plan to extend traditional authority into new resettlement areas (discussed below).

This book has also explored the micro-relations of gender in a resettlement context in an attempt to understand aspects of women's agency, identity, and relationships that have not commonly been explored in feminist analysis of women in the region. The work that women put into their marriages through the use of husband-taming herbs reveals both their desperation in the face of high rates of mar-ital instability in the context of few economic and social alternatives and key ways that women take up gender struggle and express their agency. The investigation of husband-taming herbs in these pages has revealed the importance of both female friendships and female rivalry in how women perceive and carry out the task of protecting their marriages. Finally, as with the investigation of women's rela-tionship to arable land, women's relationship to these herbs is embedded in cultural institutions and understandings that are cur-rently highly dynamic and contested. The healers' analysis of how the use of husband-taming herbs has become dislodged from the customary practice that involved the extended family offers insight into the contours of the instability of marriage in the current context and the types of strategies that women view as worth pursuing.

Finally, to return to the macro-context of land reform in Zimbabwe, we find that the magnitude of the current crisis is difficult to over-state. As outlined in detail in chapter 1, the land issue in Zimbabwe is at the centre of a political and economic crisis, the outcome of which only time will tell. It is important to realize, however, that a large-scale redistribution of land is occurring in the midst of the crisis. Where are the women in this process? It is my hope that this study will remind all those who have an interest in Zimbabwe's land crisis and changing land reform program that gender relations and struggles are strongly implicated in these issues. Will the land reform process reinforce women's inequitable relationship to land or provide them with new opportunities to improve their position? Important gains were made for women in the first stage of resettlement, despite overarching structural problems. Will all of this be lost as the new dynamics of the land process emerge?

One recent report based on fieldwork in late 2002 indicates that women have not received their fair share of land in the fast-track process (Sachikonye 2003). Indeed, under the fast track process about 300,000 small-scale farmers and 30,000 black commercial farmers have received entitlement to land since 2000. Less than 20 per cent of these were women. In-depth fieldwork is needed to determine the emerging gender relations of land and agriculture in this new context.

The Women and Land Lobby Group (WLLG) was formed in 1998 by Zimbabwean women activists committed to the land issue. Since 1998, they have lobbied government to include women's interests in its design of land reform (WLLG 2000). WLLG has critiqued government policy papers published since 1998 (Zimbabwe 1998, 1999, 2000). As a result of these efforts, the latest government document on land reform policy does include some response to WLLG's concerns. The new document (Zimbabwe 2001) sets out the various models to be pursued in the post-fast-track context. Model A1 contains two variants meant to meet the needs of the land hungry in rural areas. The first is the "villagized variant," wherein people will settle in villages and the state will provide services, much like the old Model A family farm model. The second is the "self-contained variant," wherein farmers will settle in self-contained plots and be largely responsible for the infrastructural development of their farms. This is much like the model that was discussed in the mid-1990s (see chapter 1). It is under the self-contained variant of Model A1 that we see a nod to WLLG's concerns. Here, one article in the document (article 3.2.3.5 Land Tenure Arrangements) contains this statement: "The land tenure system offers each family a ninety-nine-year lease with option to purchase. Land leases and title deeds for married couples should be in both spouses' names" (Zimbabwe 2001: 13). A similar clause appears under Model A2, which covers small, medium and large-scale commercial settlement schemes.

WLLG (2001) has responded to this new document. While the organization acknowledges that the inclusion of the article on joint leases and titles appears to represent a significant victory, WLLG sees many remaining hurtles. First, it is still the practice to follow the old way of writing only the husband's name on permits and titles, and hence a crucial problem emerges regarding the implementation of new policies in the context of rapid settlement under the fast-track process. When challenged on this problem in a public forum, the minister of lands, agriculture and rural resettlement, Dr J. Made, was reported to have said, "'Since the family is traditionally made up of two partners, government cannot say which partner should come forward to apply for land.' He was of the view that such specifics must be left to the families to decide. Participants had problems with this position because they felt it is not gender sensitive and fails to deal with the obstacles faced by women in land ownership due to traditional views on the notion of family" (WLLG 2000: 9).

Second, as most rural women do not have registered marriages, they cannot insist that this new provision apply to them. This point could be used against them if they push for the implementation of joint permits and leases. Further, there is no provision with respect to infrastructure under the fast-track process – an omission that increases women settlers' burden, as they carry the heaviest load in gathering fuel and water in undeveloped home sites. In addition, the fast-track process is characterized by violence and a lack of planning, conditions that work to marginalize women as new settlers and favour war veterans. Indeed, there has been generalized disorder and violence in many rural areas of the country related both to the fast-track process and the crackdown on political opposition:

More recently, state-sanctioned violence that accompanied the 2003 pre-election campaign, the presidential elections, and the seizure of white-owned farms has taken an especially heavy toll on women and children. It is alleged that wives and daughters who sympathized with the Movement for Democratic Change (MDC) or who were connected to MDC supporters, as well as women farm workers were victimized by ZANU youth brigades. Although the youth brigades were particularly intent on silencing vocal opposition to the ruling party, who were disproportionately male, there was clearly a gendered dimension to their violence. Women believed to be associated with the opposition were not beaten, but were instead often raped or gang raped by members of the youth brigades and state functionaries. (Osirim 2003)

The reported incidents of state-sanctioned rape were so widespread that Osirim concludes that "public, state-sanctioned violence against women has become a reality in Zimbabwe today" (Osirim 2003).

A further problem is that it is unclear what the tenure arrangements will be for the villagized variant of the Model A1. No clause on this issue is included in the government document. It may be that most new settlements will be of this type, although the fieldwork has not yet been done to determine this. If these areas are to be managed by traditional authorities, this will likely go against women's interests. Indeed the role of traditional authorities and practices in the shaping of the land reform process is potentially a big worry. First, there is the emerging discourse on restitution, which, unlike in the South African case, did not figure significantly in the earlier stages of Zimbabwe's land reform process. This is a discourse that marginalizes women. Traditional leaders are coming forward with claims to specific land areas on the basis of their sacredness to their culture or because their ancestors came from those places (Marongwe 2002; Chironga 2000). Meanwhile, the government showed its intention to strengthen traditional authorities by enacting the Traditional Leaders' Act, 1998 (implemented 1 January 2000). This act makes provision for village-level affairs and gives the responsibility for the allocation of land and land use and regulation to traditional leaders. As patriarchal and patrilineal institutions (see chapter 6), traditional authorities are not likely to entertain women's interests if they contradict traditional practices. Legal provisions that might help women in their struggle for change remain weak. The Land Act and the inheritance bills still do not deal with the land inheritance issue, which means that women who are widowed will continue to be vulnerable to the loss of land through customary practices.

This leads to what the WLLG considers the most fundamental legal issue – the need to amend the Zimbabwean constitution. The constitution represents a threat to women because it does not prohibit discrimination on the basis of sex. Consequently, women may be discriminated against on the basis of customary law and practices. As discussed in chapter 2, women's equality rights, guaranteed under the Legal Age of Majority Act (LAMA 1982), were successfully challenged in an inheritance case argued before the Zimbabwean Supreme Court in 1999. Effectively, women's equality rights can be disregarded in favour of customary laws and practices that discriminate against them.

The contradiction between customary law, practices, and attitudes and modern individual rights appears to be central to the complex battleground for women and land in Southern Africa. South Africa is facing a similar set of contradictions in its land reform process, although there are many differences in history and context between the two countries (Rangan and Gilmartin 2002; Walker 2002). The South African state seeks to guarantee individual rights through its constitution, which ensures non-discrimination on the basis of sex. It also targets women as a special group in its land reform policy. At the same time, however, the state supports the right of traditional authorities to allocate land under some contexts of the land reform process. These traditional authorities follow practices that allocate land mainly to married men, much like customary practices in Zimbabwe. Thus, women's constitutional rights are violated, and as a result, a gendered struggle in relation to land reform has emerged in South Africa (Rangan and Gilmartin 2002). More generally, when communities agitate for progress on the land reform issue in South Africa, women are often marginalized by the customary institutions and practices around which communities organize. As Walker states, "The strength of patriarchal attitudes, coupled to the government's apparent reluctance to intervene too actively to curtail the powers of traditional authorities at the local level, is another constraint on land reform that will not be quickly resolved" (Walker 2002: 88).

The Zimbabwean experience indicates a seeming intractability in the conflict between African customary practice and a modern, rights-based legal framework. While the Zimbabwean government clearly has not been as committed to the inclusion of equality rights for women as the South African state appears to have been, both states face a similar post-colonial challenge. Both are attempting to forge a nationalist land reform process from within the colonial legacy of a dual legal system and historical race-based injustice. If such an endeavour were not difficult enough, it must also be done within a modern context where women demand equal rights and opportunities.

This study of Zimbabwe has demonstrated how crucial the role of the state is in the process of bringing in land reform that is fair to women; it has also shown, however, that the local and micro-dynamics of gender relations in households and in communities have their own momentum and that women's struggles will continue far beyond any victories of policy reform. While it is important to monitor laws and policies and debate the pros and cons of different tenure regimes for women's interests, it is equally important to understand the depth and complexity of women's struggles within their families and communities.

In all, the strategies for promoting women's entitlement to land that utilize claims to equality rights and appeals to the state to act as an agent of change have clear limitations. The equality claim has fallen on rough ground as we have seen, given the strength of counter-sociocultural forces at all levels, from households to top state functionaries, to reinstate what is presented as traditional gender relations. This makes it very difficult to integrate gender justice into the justice discourses surrounding land reform, whether they utilize race or class arguments. The strategy of appealing to the state is consequently hampered from the outset, but it is also handicapped by the incomplete power of the state to impose social change through law or policy, particularly in rural areas, as shown by WLSA's work (see chapter 2) and by the evidence presented in this book.

However, there is another element of the land reform debate that tends to operate without regard to women's claims to land. This is the aspect that recognizes the importance of the economic value of land as used in agriculturally productive ways. What appears to be at stake is the transformation of the social category of "women" to include not only a modern, rights-based identity on an equal footing with men in terms of access to land, but also an identity as productive farmers or eligible subjects for modern development. The women's land-rights movement throughout the region is fully engaged with this problem, noting that despite the many disadvantages, women have proven themselves to be productive and efficient farmers. However, secure entitlement to land must be accompanied with improvement in both economic resources, such as access to credit and labour, and social resources, such as training, technical support, and, most difficult of all, social transformation (WLLG 2001a).

CONCLUSION

Unfortunately for the cause of women's right to land, it appears that women as subjects entitled to land, whether justified under an equal-rights or a productivity framework, are powerfully marginalized in a context where "African patriarchies have hardened" (Msimang 2002: 13), both within the state and at local levels of traditional authority and the family. The state indicates its lack of support for women's land rights indirectly, through the proposed involvement of traditional authorities in land allocation in the new land reform process. This indicates that the state does not recognize women as having equal rights to land; nor does it see them as modern producers in their own right, since traditional authorities are unlikely to allow women to achieve primary rights to land. Current state policy also indicates that the operations of local patriarchies will likely be even less encumbered by state control than was previously the case.

More directly, the state balks at taking a strong leading role in the extension of modern rights to women and retreats before the authority of the family in the land allocation processes (such as resettlement policy) that it ostensibly controls. These moves signal state retreat from a program of gender justice and hence raise serious questions about the role of the state as a vehicle in support of women's struggle for land rights. They may also signal the abandonment of a coherent modernizing strategy in relation to agricultural production. Indeed, as argued in chapter 1, the current dynamics may be mostly reflective of state attempts to garner political support and economic power through the strategic allocation of land to key groups. The exclusion of rural, small-scale farming women from these groups comes with few political costs at this moment. Perhaps echoing the colonial state's curtailing of women's freedom of movement as one means of gaining male leaders' cooperation in colonial times (see Schmidt 1992a; Barnes 1999), the contemporary state, by courting the support of traditional authorities and other beneficiaries of local patriarchies, is sacrificing justice for women in a bid to shore up its own power. Feminists in Zimbabwe have every reason to fear that the small gains that resettlement women have enjoyed and that may be promised by new and future state policies are deeply compromised by the current struggles for land in Zimbabwe.

In the hurried and often violent fast-track process, women have to deal with the micro-dynamics of entitlement, which include formal and informal institutions and follow both customary and state-designed practices and policies in a highly masculinized social field of war veterans, traditional authorities, and state agents. Women must do this, too, within the larger processes of race- and class-based conflict and the political struggle of a state in crisis. Indeed, the state crisis of today strongly indicates the necessity of escaping the bounds of exclusionary thinking and practice currently ruling land reform as a result of the crisis. A comprehensive feminist vision should interrogate the multiple exclusions in this process, not only of women farmers, but also of farm workers and the urban poor, as these exclusions delineate the inequality, corruption, disenfranchisement, and development crisis that characterize Zimbabwe.[2] While small gains may be made through changes in state policy, far-reaching change for women will require a broader project of social justice and democratic transformation.

Notes

CHAPTER ONE

1 "Land Issue a time bomb: Chiwewe," *Herald*, 29 July 1996.
2 Kriger (1992) takes a different angle on this, arguing that peasants were less radicalized in this period than historians of the war have suggested. Instead, she argues that "peasant resistance" was in large part imposed by guerrillas, often through coercive means. Dictates to resist practices such as contour ridging were part of this.
3 See Akwabi-Ameyaw 1990 for a comparative analysis of Model A and Model B schemes and an analysis of the overall failure of the cooperative model.
4 Interview with district administrator, Wedza Rural District Council, 18 February 1997.
5 Interview, Magamba Secondary School headmaster, Wedza, 7 October 1996.
6 "Resettlement gets low priority: ZFU," *Herald*, 7 August 1995: 1; "Cost-recovery measures sought for resettlement," *Herald*, 22 February 1996. To put this in the depressing context of state spending on the maintenance of the personal class interests of its chosen elite, consider the $6 million spent on a new mansion for Grace Mugabe, the new wife of the president ("Grace lands a $6m house," *Zimbabwe Independent*, 11–17 October 1996: 1).

7 See also "Comment: Landmark decision," *Sunday Mail*, 18 August 1996: 10. In this editorial, the issue of granting long-term leases to small-scale farmers is linked to the drive to indigenize commercial farming and the need to ensure that "[b]lack farmers, especially those under the auspices of the Zimbabwe Farmers' Union and the Indigenous Commercial Farmers' Union ... as well as graduates of agricultural colleges" will be given the "first opportunity" on newly available farm land.

8 "Land shortage problem deteriorates," *Sunday Mail*, 16 June 1996; "Resettlement funds too low," *Herald*, 3 August 1995: 12. Another article ("3 million ha bought for resettlement since 1980," *Herald*, 26 November 1996: 9) unaccountably reduces the figure to 80,000 families waiting. "State to compulsorily acquire 27 farms," *Herald*, 29 December 1995: 1; "Farmers turn abusive over land issue," *Sunday Mail*, 23 June 1996: 1.

9 See "No cash for resettlement programme as State acquires 25 farms," *Herald*, 4 April 1996: 1; "Land re-distribution hit by lack of funds," *Herald*, 21 April 1996: 9; "Zimbabwe and Britain still discuss resettlement funding," *Herald*, 21 May 1996; "Land programme supported," *Herald*, 20 June 1996; "State to get British help to acquire land," *Herald*, 7 September 1996.

10 Interview with Sengezi Resettlement officer, 17 July 1996; Interview with district administrator of Wedza District (18 February 1997).

11 The 1992 Census put the annual population growth rate at 3.14 per cent (Central Statistical Office 1994). A study released by the Blair Research Institute and Oxford University's Centre for the Epidemiology of Infectious Disease predicts that AIDS-related deaths will reach such high proportions in Zimbabwe that the population will stay steady over the next three decades. The AIDS-related death rate was estimated at about 500 deaths per week in the mid-1990s, in a population of nearly 12 million. The effects of decreasing the population growth rate through this means are predicted to be devastating for the economy and the society, as those of prime economically active age will be struck down ("Static population size does not mean less environmental problems," *Sunday Mail Magazine*, 2 March 1997: 10).

12 Interviews with former ward councillor, September 1996, and field assistant.

13 "Land shortage problem deteriorates," *Sunday Mail*, 16 June 1996. See also "Resettlement must depend on productivity: seminar," *Herald*, 16 April 1996: 1; "Comment: Landmark decision," *Sunday Mail*,

18 August 1996: 10; "Residents with resources sought for resettlement," *Herald*, 20 August 1996: 7.

14 Interview with Wedza District administrator, 18 February 1997.

15 K. Kangai, minister of lands and water development, 28 May 1997, speaking at the Consultative Conference on Land in Zimbabwe, convened by the NGO ZERO and held at the ZESA Training Centre, Harare, 27–28 May 1997. See also "Big change for resettlement areas," *Herald*, 7 August 1995: 7; "Major changes in land tenure," *Herald*, 16 August 1996: 1.

16 "New plan to groom communal farmers," *Herald*, 7 October 1995: 1; "Trusts proposed for communal land," *Herald*, 24 December 1995: 1; "Scheme set to ease resettlement woes," *Herald*, 24 January 1996.

17 "Cost-recovery measures sought for resettlement," *Herald*, 22 February 1996.

18 "Comment: Resettlement must have future in mind," *Herald*, 20 October 1995: 10.

19 "25 farms acquired for resettlement," *Herald*, 4 June 1996: 1; "Land shortage problem deteriorates," *Sunday Mail*, 16 June 1996.

20 See, for example, "Armed squatters beat farm workers," *Globe and Mail* (Canada), 24 April 2000: A8; "Mugabe raises spectre of martial law; US moots sanctions after attacks on white farms grow," *Guardian Weekly* (UK), 16–22 August 2001: 4.

21 C. Chimakure, "New Controversy over Land," *Zimbabwe Mirror*, 24 November 2000 (africaonline); Moyo 2000.

22 "Zimbabwe: IRIN interview with land expert Sam Moyo," *Integrated Regional Information Networks* <www.reliefweb.int/IRIN/sa/countrystories/Zimbabwe/200108014.phtml>.

23 Chris McGreal, "Mugabe raises spectre of martial law," *Guardian Weekly*, 16–22 August 2001: 4.

24 "Politically related deaths now over 150," *Zimbabwe Independent*, 4 October 2002.

25 "Go now, farmers told, as Zimbabwe sets deadline," *New Zealand Herald*, 20 August 2001 (online).

26 Basildon Peta, "Zimbabwe court cancels eviction orders on 54 farmers," *Independent* (UK), in ZWNEWS, 29 August 2002.

27 "Zimbabwe farmers near Botswana border ordered out," *VOA News*, in ZWNEWS, 2 October 2002.

28 "Zimbabwe changes land law," *Mail and Guardian* (SA), 29 January 2004, in ZWNEWS, 29 January 2004.

29 "Zimbabwe ban extended," *BBC News*, in ZWNEWS, 16 March 2003.

30 "'The time is auspicious to lift the sanctions on Zimbabwe,'" *Business Day* (SA), in ZWNEWS, 12 February 2003.

31 "Mugabe quits Commonwealth," *Guardian* (UK), 8 December 2003, in ZWNEWS, 8 December 2003.

32 "GTZ bails out," *Zimbabwe Independent*, in ZWNEWS, 27 September 2002.

33 See discussion above. Also, for one of many examples of government friends moving onto former white commercial farms, see Adam Nathan and David Leppard, "Sainsbury's supplied by Mugabe aide," *Sunday Times* (UK), in ZWNEWS, 21 October 2002.

CHAPTER TWO

1 Cited in Cheater and Gaidzanwa 1996: 200.

2 For a discussion of the politics of labelling among African female scholars, see Nnaemeka 1998. Many scholars reject "feminist" as a white Western label and prefer the "womanist" label as promoted by many African American scholars. As there is no consensus on this question, I include both here.

3 See, for example, Larsson et al. 1998; McFadden 1999; Meena 1992; Nnaemeka 1997, 1998; and the journal *Southern African Feminist Review* (*SAFERE*). Important exceptions to this include Oyewùmí 1997, which rejects "gender" and, indeed, "men" and "women" as useful descriptive and analytic categories. Oyewùmí argues that age/seniority was the most important social organizing principle among the Yoruba in pre-colonial times and that gender was a European imposition.

4 See Schmidt 1992a and b, Jeater 1993, Barnes 1992, and Ranchod-Nilsson 1992 for some of the key writing on colonial times, and Sylvester 2000, Gaidzanwa 1995, and the many writers engaged with below for writing on post-colonial times.

5 The continual insertion of "woman" in quotation marks is distracting and is not retained after the point of the constructedness of the category is made.

6 My focus on women does not mean that women are conflated with gender. Men and masculinity are also produced in complex and contradictory ways that other scholars are beginning to explore in African contexts (see especially Epprecht 1998 and in press, and Kesby 1999 on Zimbabwe, and Morrell 1998 and 2001 and Murray and Roscoe 1998 for collections on Africa).

7 See Rutherford 2001b for a discussion of these patterns in relation to female commercial farm workers, Stewart et al. 2000 on women and

justice delivery, and Gaidzanwa 1995, Pankhurst and Jacobs 1988, and Goebel 1999a on women's access to land and other resources.

8 Sylvester 2000 (71–86) outlines several coexisting and often contradictory "regimes of truth" (after Foucault) in post-colonial Zimbabwe, including the liberal-pragmatic, the socialist, the insider strength (authoritarian), and the aid regimes that shape power relations and the meanings of progress.

9 See Murray 1981 and 1987, Gordon 1981, Gay 1980, Epprecht 2000, and Malahleha 1985 on the extreme case of male migration in Lesotho; Berheide and Segal 1994 on Malawi; Moore and Vaughan 1994 on Zambia; Davison 1997 for historical overview of Southern Africa; Pankhurst and Jacobs 1988, Jacobs and Howard 1987, Schmidt 1992a and b, Gaidzanwa 1995, Chimedza 1988, and Kesby 1999 on Zimbabwe; Bryceson 1997, Jiggins 1989, Brydon and Chant 1989, Hansen 1992, and Meena 1992 for general discussions of the issue in Africa.

10 The term "Shona" is discussed later in this chapter.

11 Such marriages were often called *mapoto*, literally meaning a marriage with pots. The implication was that the union was informal, about living together in a home, the woman doing the domestic work for the man, without all the conventional trappings, such as payment of *lobola*, or pride price, of a proper marriage (Amanor-Wilks 1996).

12 See Schmidt 1992a; Barnes and Win 1992; Barnes 1999; Horn 1994.

13 See "Never to own the land they till" (ZWRCN 1996: 6–8); Moyo 1995; Stewart 1992.

14 See, for example, ZWRCN 1996, News Bulletin; ZWRCN 1994. Some female politicians have also been vocal about this issue. See, for example, comments of Minister of National Affairs, Employment Creation and Co-operatives Thenjiwe Lesabe in "Laws needed to give women access to land," *Herald*, 16 May 1996.

15 Jonathan Manthorpe, "Women lose fight for equal rights in Zimbabwe," *Vancouver Sun*, 22 May 1999: A1, A2. See also "Supreme Court hits out at women," *Zimbabwe Independent*, 18 June 1999 (online).

16 See ZWRCN, "Cutting Edge," *Zimbabwe Independent*, 8 October 1999 (online); and a special section in *SAFERE*, 4 (1) (2000), which documents Zimbabwean women's engagement with the constitutional review process.

17 See Stewart et al. 2000 below, McFadden, Jirira, and Osirim as examples of Zimbabwean feminist scholars. All four of these Zimbabwean women have been active as both academics and activists;

they write from a critical stance vis-à-vis the state and increasingly about issues of sexuality and violence.

18 See also Amadiume 1997; Lewis 2000; Nkulukeko 1987; Nnaemeka 1997; Wanzala 1998.

19 "Shona" is a label for a number of linguistically related (but distinct) groups in the region covering most of present-day Zimbabwe and large parts of Mozambique. The term may first have been used by invading Ndebele, but was later adopted by colonialists. Different sub-groups include Zezuru in central Zimbabwe (including Wedza District, the study site), Korekore in the north, the Karanga and Kalanga in the south, and the Manyika and Ndau in the east (Bourdillon 1987: 16–19).

20 Interview with the headmaster of Magamba Secondary School, Wedza, 28 August 1996. This informant is of the ruling Jena totem.

21 "Poverty burden heavy in Communal Areas," *Herald*, September 1995.

22 See, for example, "No development," *Herald*, 7 August 1996: 4. In a letter from Chinyika resettlement area, a settler laments that "[t]his place is hundred percent underdeveloped and there seems to be no hope of improvement … The roads are no better than dongas and pits such that bus operators are deterred from applying for permits to use the road."

CHAPTER FIVE

1 K. Kangai, minister of lands and water development, speaking at the Consultative Conference on Land in Zimbabwe, convened by the NGO ZERO and held at the ZESA Training Center, Harare, 27–28 May 1997. The minister's speech was delivered on 28 May 1997.

2 Women and Land Working Group, Consultative Conference on Land in Zimbabwe, convened by the NGO ZERO and held at the ZESA Training Center, Harare, 27–28 May 1997.

3 K. Kangai, minister of lands and water development, 28 May 1997. See note 1.

4 K. Kangai, minister of lands and water development. See note 1.

5 United Nations Department of Public Information, *Convention on the Elimination of All Forms of Discrimination against Women*, February 1993. As cited in Chenaux-Repond 1996: 5.

6 Women's views were voiced in a conference organized by Chenaux-Repond (see Chenaux-Repond 1996) and supported by all of Zimbabwe's major women's organizations and some human rights organizations. See also "Inheritance issue not clear for women

farmers," *Herald*, 1 December 1995, and "Apply common law on inheritance to minimize conflicts," *Herald*, 14 August 1995, for discussion of the issues in the local press.

7 See Nkala 1996. Nowhere in this lengthy discussion of recommended ways forward for sustainable development of agriculture in rural Zimbabwe are women's interests or gender relations in agriculture or resource use mentioned.

CHAPTER SIX

1 The documentary film *With These Hands: How Women Feed Africa*, made by the New Internationalist, offers an optimistic 1986 view of women's political agency in its depiction of a VIDCO meeting in a resettlement area in Zimbabwe.

2 These pressures, particularly as embodied by the Native Land Husbandry Act (1951; see chapter 1) and the policies and practices of the Forest Office in colonial times, are important topics in themselves, too broad to be discussed at length here (see Goebel 1997).

3 Traditional healers, who may be male or female, use roots and bark for different remedies and also use *muhacha* extensively. Fruits are also eaten (Drummond and Coates Palgrave 1973: 17–19).

4 These spirits are not ancestors per se but rather are translated as "mermaids" (*nzuzu*). Generally malevolent, they are thought to "take" people, who may then re-emerge as traditional healers.

5 There is no space here to go into these rules or the history of the Natural Resources Board. It is enough to say that the NRB is part of the legacy of the colonial state, operating according to Western conservationist values. While the post-independence NRB relies more on persuasion and education than did its colonial predecessor, which favoured punitive policies with respect to rule breakers, the analysis of environmental management remains largely the same.

6 If there is a history of conquest in the territory – the current ruling lineage having come from elsewhere and settled after defeating a former ruling lineage – appeasement of the original spirits may also be required (Bourdillon 1987; Lan 1985).

7 Mike Matshosh Hove, quoted in Hove and Trojanow 1996. In this work, *Guardians of the Soil*, the authors interview eleven elders from across Zimbabwe about the soil, history, and problems of the present-day leadership.

8 Sub-Chief Kadere quoted in Hove and Trojanow 1996: 102.

9 See Collins 1991 as an example of this approach and Braidotti et al. 1994, Harcourt 1994, Alaimo 1994, Jackson 1993, Joekes et al. 1994, Rocheleau et al. 1996, and Sturgeon 1997 for analyses of its limitations.

10 See Goebel 2002b for a more thorough examination of women, gender, and environment theory.

CHAPTER SEVEN

1 I use "healers" as a general label to embrace both the *n'angas* (traditional healers who are consulted about a wide range of illnesses and problems and who incorporate divination skills through their link with a healing spirit who assists them with ancestor consultation and often – but not always – also administer herbal medicines) and the specialists who deal only with husband-taming herbs and are not *n'angas* in the broader sense (see Bourdillon 1987: 147–69 for a discussion of the distinction between *n'angas* and healers without divination powers). Both types of healers were interviewed in this project.

2 Hannan 1984: 396.

3 At the time of the research, I could not drum up interest in lab analysis of the plants at the University of Zimbabwe. Perhaps future research will include this.

4 WAG was started in the early 1980s as a women's organization devoted to promoting women's rights, especially in rural areas, through outreach initiatives and networking. WAG hosts periodic national conferences at the University of Zimbabwe in Harare, to which rural women members are bussed to hear about developments in women's legal status and approaches to the social problems women face such as violence and health risks.

5 A *tokoloshi* is described as a dwarf-like creature kept by some traditional healers and witches that imparts magical powers to the keeper. The creature requires human blood for food and sometimes many wives, whom the creature visits for sex at night.

6 "Witchcraft" must be understood as separate from the practice of herbal medicine. Genuine traditional healers use herbs for their medicinal and symbolic properties to treat physical and psychological illnesses, often with effective results.

7 "Harsh anti-witchcraft laws proposed," *Sunday Mail*, 7 July 1996.

8 Bourdillon also notes that this distinction is not rigid; indeed, the same word is used for both sorcerers and witches (*varoyi*), but Shona often make the distinction through context or description of the person's

attributes, and people respond differently to the two activities
(Bourdillon 1987: 181).

9 "Harsh anti-witchcraft laws proposed," *Sunday Mail*, 7 July 1996.
10 Such a case happened right on our doorstep at the secondary school
   where I stayed during my fieldwork in 1995–97.

CHAPTER EIGHT

1 See also "137 Harare girls raped in January: activist," AFP 12 February
  2004, in ZWNEWS, 12 February 2004.
2 The WLLG has begun looking at the gendered dynamics of urban
  agriculture in Zimbabwe in an important expansion of the usual
  preoccupation of the investigation of "women and land" (see
  <www.ruaf.org/no4/18_wo_zim.htm>). Marongwe noted that the year
  2000 land occupations included occupations of land (including commercial farms) near urban centres, as many urban dwellers have no
  land for housing. He notes that "policy and decision-makers whose
  view is that land reform was meant to benefit the rural populations
  and, therefore a 'non-urban issue' have wrong[ly] interpreted the
  process" (Marongwe 2002: 41).

References

Akwabi-Ameyaw, K. 1990. "The Political Economy of Agricultural Resettlement and Rural Development in Zimbabwe: The Performance of Family Farms and Producer Co-operatives." *Human Organization* 49:320–38.

Alaimo, Stacy. 1994. "Cyborg and Ecofeminist Interventions: Challenges for an Environmental Feminism." *Feminist Studies* 20 (1): 133–53.

Alexander, J. 1994. "State, Peasantry and Resettlement in Zimbabwe." *Review of African Political Economy* 6:325–45.

Amadiume, Ifi. 1997. *Re-inventing Africa: Matriarchy, Religion and Culture.* London and New York: Zed Books.

Amanor-Wilks, Dede. 1996. "Invisible Hands: Women in Zimbabwe's Commercial Farm Sector." *Southern Africa Feminist Review* 2 (1): 37–56.

Andersson, Jens A. 1999. "The Politics of Land Scarcity: Land Disputes in Save Communal Area, Zimbabwe." *Journal of Southern African Studies* 25 (4): 553–78.

Armstrong, A., and W. Ncube, eds. 1987. *Women and Law in Southern Africa.* Harare: Zimbabwe Publishing House.

Barnes, Theresa. 1992. "The Fight for Control of Women's Mobility in Colonial Zimbabwe." *Signs* 17 (3): 586–608.

– 1999. *"We Women Worked So Hard": Gender, Labour and Social Reproduction in Colonial Harare, Zimbabwe, 1930–1956.* Portsmouth, NH: Heinemann.

Barnes, Theresa, and Everjoyce Win. 1992. *To Live a Better Life: An Oral History of Women in the City of Harare, 1930–70.* Harare: Baobab Books.

Beach, David N. 1980. *The Shona and Zimbabwe 900–1850.* Gweru, Zimbabwe: Mambo Press.

Beinart, Willian. 1984. "Soil Erosion, Conservationism and Ideas about Development: A Southern African Exploration, 1900–1960." *Journal of Southern African Studies* 11 (1): 52–83.

– 1989. "Introduction: The Politics of Colonial Conservation." *Journal of Southern African Studies* 15 (2): 143–62.

Berheide, Catherine White, and Marcia Texler Segal. 1994. "Controlling Less Land, Producing Less Food: The Fate of Female-Headed Households in Malawi." In *Women, the Family and Policy: A Global Perspective*, edited by Esther Ngan-ling Chow and Catherine White Berheide, 145–62. New York: State University of New York Press.

Bhebe, Ngwabi. 1979. *Christianity and Traditional Religion in Western Zimbabwe, 1859–1923*. London: Longman.

Bhebe, N., and T. Ranger, eds. 1995. *Soldiers in Zimbabwe's Liberation War*. London: James Currey; Portsmouth, NH: Heinemann.

Bond, Patrick, and Masimba Manyanya. 2002. *Zimbabwe's Plunge: Exhausted Nationalism, Neoliberalism and the Search for Social Justice*. Pietermaritzburg: University of Natal Press.

Bourdillon, M.F.C. 1987. *The Shona Peoples*. Rev. ed. Gwere: Mambo Press.

– 1993. *Where Are the Ancestors? Changing Culture in Zimbabwe*. Harare: University of Zimbabwe Publications.

Braidotti, Rosi; Ewa Charkiewicz; Sabine Häusler; and Saskia Wieringa. 1994. *Women, the Environment and Sustainable Development: Towards a Theoretical Synthesis*. London: Zed Books in association with INSTRAW.

Bratton, Michael. 1994. "Land Distribution, 1980–1990." In *Zimbabwe's Agricultural Revolution*, edited by M. Rukuni and C.K. Eicher, 70–86. Gweru: University of Zimbabwe Publications.

Bruijn, Mirjam de; Ineke van Halsema; and Heleen van den Hombergh, eds. 1997. *Gender and Land Use: Diversity in Environmental Practice*. Amsterdam: Thela Publishers.

Bryceson, D.F., ed. 1997. *Women Wielding the Hoe: Lessons from Rural Africa for Feminist Theory and Development Practice*. Oxford and Washington, DC: Berg Publishers.

Brydon, Lynne, and S. Chant. 1989. *Women in the Third World: Gender Issues in Rural and Urban Areas*. Hants, England: Edward Eldgar Publishing.

Cawthorne, Maya. 1999. "The Third Chimurenga." In *Reflections on Gender Issues in Africa*, edited by P. McFadden, 55–83. Harare: Southern Africa Political Economy Series (SAPES) Publishers.

Central Statistics Office (Zimbabwe). 1994. *Census 1992: Zimbabwe National Report*. Harare: Government Printers.

Chavunduka, Gordon L. 1982. *Report on the Commission of Inquiry into the Agricultural Industry* ("The Chavunduka Report"). Harare: Government Printers.

– 1997. *Traditional Medicine in Modern Zimbabwe*. Harare: University of Zimbabwe Publications.

Cheater, A. 1981. "Women and Their Participation in Commercial Agricultural Production: The Case of Medium-Scale Freehold in Zimbabwe." *Development and Change* 12 (3): 349–72.

– 1984. *Idioms of Accumulation: Rural Development and Class Formation among Freeholders in Zimbabwe*. Gweru: Mambo Press.

– 1990. "The Ideology of 'Communal' Land Tenure in Zimbabwe: Mythogenesis Enacted?" *Africa* 60 (2): 188–206.

Cheater, A., and R.B. Gaidzanwa. 1996. "Citizenship in Neo-Patrilineal States: Gender and Mobility in Southern Africa." *Journal of Southern African Studies* 22 (2): 189–200.

Chenaux-Repond, M. 1993. *Gender Biased Land-Use Rights in Model A Resettlement Schemes of Mashonaland, Zimbabwe*. Harare: Rubicon Zimbabwe.

– ed. 1996. *Women Farmers' Position: Our Response to the Land Tenure Commission Report*. Harare: Friedrich-Ebert-Stiftung, Rubicon Zimbabwe.

Chimedza, Ruvimbo. 1988. "Women's Access to and Control over Land: The Case of Zimbabwe." Working Paper AEE 10/88, Department of Agricultural Economics and Extension, University of Zimbabwe.

Chironga, S. 2000. "Rural Communities' Perspectives on Zimbabwe's Land Reforms: A Focus on Land Invasions." Seminar Proceedings 37. Workshop organized by ZERO Regional Environment Organisation and Friedrich-Ebert-Stiftung and Humanistic Institute for Co-operation with Development Countries, 3–4 May 2000, ZESA National Training Centre, Harare.

Chow, E., and Berheide, C., eds. 1994. *Women, the Family and Policy: A Global Perspective*. New York: State University of New York Press.

Christiansen, R.E. 1993. "Implementing Strategies for the Rural Economy: Lesson from Zimbabwe, Options for South Africa." *World Development* 21 (9): 1549–66.

Civic, Diane, and David Wilson. 1996. "Dry Sex in Zimbabwe and Implications for Condom Use." *Social Science and Medicine* 42 (1): 91–8.

Cliffe, Lionel. 1988a. "The Conservation Issue in Zimbabwe." *Review of African Political Economy* 42:48–58.

– 1988b. "The Prospects for Agricultural Transformation in Zimbabwe." In C. Stoneman (ed) *Zimbabwe's Prospects: Issues of Race, Class, State and Capital in Southern Africa*, edited by C. Stoneman, 309–25. Basingstoke: Macmillan.

Collins, Jane L. 1991. "Women and the Environment: Social Reproduction and Sustainable Development." In *The Women and International Development Annual*, edited by R.S. Gallin and A. Ferguson, 33–58. Vol. 2. Boulder, CO: Westview Press.

Comoroff, Jean, and John Comoroff. 1991. *Of Revelation and Revolution: Christianity, Colonialism, and Consciousness in South Africa.* Chicago: University of Chicago Press.

Dashwood, Hevina S. 2000. *Zimbabwe: The Political Economy of Transition.* Toronto: University of Toronto Press.

Davison, Jean, ed. 1988. *Agriculture, Women and Land: The African Experience.* Boulder, CO: Westview Press.

– 1997. *Gender, Lineage and Ethnicity in Southern Africa.* Boulder, CO: Westview Press.

Dodd, Elizabeth. 1997. "The Mamas and the Papas: Goddess Worship, the Kogi Indians, and Ecofeminism." *NWSA Journal* 9 (3): 77–88.

Drinkwater, Michael. 1989. "Technical Development and Peasant Impoverishment: Land Use Policy in Zimbabwe's Midlands Province." *Journal of Southern African Studies* 15 (2): 287–305.

Drummond, R.B., and K. Coates Palgrave. 1973. *Common Trees of the Highveld.* Salisbury, Rhodesia: Longman.

Dzingirai, Vupenyu. 2003. "The New Scramble for the African Countryside." *Development and Change* 34 (2): 243–63.

Elliott, Jennifer. 1991. "Environmental Degradation, Soil Conservation and the Colonial and Post-Colonial State in Rhodesia/Zimbabwe." In *Colonialism and Development in the Contemporary World*, edited by C. Dixon and M. Hefferman, 72–91. London: Mansell.

Epprecht, Marc. 1998. "The 'Unsaying' of Indigenous Homosexualities in Zimbabwe: Mapping a Blindspot in an African Masculinity." *Journal of Southern African Studies* 24 (4): 631–51.

– 2000. *"This matter of women is getting very bad": Gender, Development and Politics in Colonial Lesotho.* Pietermaritzburg: University of Natal Press.

– Forthcoming. *Hungochani: The History of a Dissident Sexuality in Southern Africa.* Montreal and Kingston: McGill-Queen's University Press.

Fapohunda, Eleanor F. 1988. "The Non-pooling Household: A Challenge to Theory." In *A Home Divided: Women and Income in the Third World*, edited by D. Dwyer and J. Bruce, 143–54. Stanford: Stanford University Press.

Folbre, Nancy. 1988. "The Black Four of Hearts: Towards a New Paradigm of Household Economics." In *A Home Divided: Women and Income in the Third World*, edited by D. Dwyer and J. Bruce, 248–62. Stanford: Stanford University Press.

Fortmann, Louise. 1996. "Gendered Knowledge: Rights and Space in Two Zimbabwe Villages." In *Feminist Political Ecology: Global Issues and Local Experiences*, edited by D. Rocheleau et al., 211–23. London: Routledge.

Fortmann, L., and J. Bruce. 1993. "Tenure and Gender Issues in Forest Policy." In *Living with Trees: Policies for Forestry Management in Zimbabwe*, edited by P.N. Bradley and K. McNamara, 199–210. Washington, DC: World Bank Technical Paper No. 210.

Fortmann, L., and N. Nabane. 1992. "The Fruits of Their Labours: Gender, Property and Trees in Mhondoro District." Centre for Applied Social Sciences, University of Zimbabwe. Occasional Paper Series – NRM, 6/1992.

Gaidzanwa, R. 1995. "Land and the Economic Empowerment of Women: A Gendered Analysis." *Southern African Feminist Review*, 1 (1): 1–12.

Gay, Judith. 1980. "Basotho Women's Options: A Study of Marital Careers in Rural Lesotho." Unpublished PHD dissertation, Cambridge University.

Geisler, Gisela. 1995. "Troubled Sisterhood: Women and Politics in Southern Africa. Case studies from Zambia, Zimbabwe and Botswana." *African Affairs* 94:545–78.

Goebel, A. 1997. "'No Spirits Control the Trees': History, Culture and Gender in the Social Forest in a Zimbabwean Resettlement Area." Unpublished PHD dissertation, Department of Sociology, University of Alberta.

– 1998. "Process, Perception and Power." Notes from "Participatory Research in a Zimbabwean Resettlement Area." *Development and Change* 29 (2): 276–305.

– 1999a. "'Here it is our land, the two of us': Women, Men and Land in a Zimbabwean Resettlement Area." *Journal of Contemporary African Studies* 17 (1) 1999: 75–96.

– 1999b. "'Then it's clear who owns the trees': Common Property and Private Control in the Social Forest in a Zimbabwean Resettlement Area." *Rural Sociology* 64 (4) 1999: 625–41.

– 2002a. "'Men these days, they are a problem': Husband-Taming Herbs and Gender Wars in Rural Zimbabwe." *Canadian Journal of African Studies* 36 (3): 460–89.

– 2002b. "Gender, Environment and Development in Southern Africa." *Canadian Journal of Development Studies* 23 (2): 293–316.

Goebel, A.; B. Campbell; B. Mukamuri; and M. Veeman. 2000. "People, Values and Woodlands: A Field Report of Emergent Themes in Interdisciplinary Research in Zimbabwe." *Agriculture and Human Values* 17 (4): 385–96.

Goebel, A., and N. Nabane. 1998. *Participatory Rural Appraisal Report: Wedza District*. Harare: German Development Cooperation (GTZ) and the Forestry Commission of Zimbabwe.

Gordon, Elizabeth. 1981. "An Analysis of the Impact of Labour Migration on the Lives of Women in Lesotho." In *African Women in the Development Process*, edited by Nici Nelson, 59–76. London: Frank Cass and Co.

Gray, Leslie, and Michael Kevane. 1999. "Diminished Access, Diverted Exclusion: Women and Land Tenure in Sub-Saharan Africa." *African Studies Review* 42 (2): 15–39.

Grove, Richard. 1989. "Scottish Missionaries, Evangelical Discourses and the Origins of Conservation Thinking in Southern Africa 1820–1900." *Journal of Southern African Studies* 15 (2): 163–87.

Guyer, Jane. 1988. "Dynamic Approaches to Domestic Budgeting: Cases and Methods from Africa." In *A Home Divided: Women and Income in the Third World*, edited by D. Dwyer and J. Bruce, 155–72. Stanford: Stanford University Press.

Hannan, M. 1984. *Standard Shona Dictionary.* Rev. ed. Harare: College Press Publishers.

Hansen, Karen Tranberg. 1992. "Introduction: Domesticity in Africa." In *African Encounters with Domesticity*, edited by Karen Tranberg Hansen, 1–33. New Brunswick, NJ: Rutgers University Press.

Harcourt, Wendy, ed. 1994. *Feminist Perspectives on Sustainable Development.* London: Zed Books.

Harts-Broekhuis, A., and H. Huisman. 2001. "Resettlement Revisited: Land Reform Results in Resource-Poor Regions in Zimbabwe." *Geoforum* 32:285–98.

Hay, Jean, and Sharon Stichter. 1984. *African Women South of the Sahara.* London and New York: Longman.

Hefner, Robert W. 1993. *Conversion to Christianity: Historical and Anthropological Perspectives on a Great Transformation.* Berkeley, Los Angeles, and Oxford: University of California Press.

Higgins, K.M., and A. Mazula. 1993. "Community Development: A National Strategy in Zimbabwe." *Community Development Journal* 28 (1): 19–30.

Hoogeveen, J.G.M., and B.H. Kinsey. 2001. "Land Reform, Growth and Equity: Emerging Evidence from Zimbabwe's Resettlement Programme – A Sequel." *Journal of Southern African Studies* 27 (1): 127–36.

Horn, Nancy E. 1994. *Cultivating Customers: Market Women in Harare, Zimbabwe.* Boulder and London: Lynne Reinner Publishers.

Hove, C., and I. Trojanow. 1996. *Guardians of the Soil: Meeting Zimbabwe's Elders.* Harare: Baobob Books; Munich: Frederking and Thaler Verlag.

Hughes, David M. 1999. "Refugees and Squatters: Immigration and the Politics of territory on the Zimbabwe-Mozambique Border." *Journal of Southern African Studies* 25 (4): 533–52.

Ibrahim, Huma. 1997. "Ontological Victimhood: 'Other' Bodies in Madness and Exile – Toward a Third World Feminist Epistemology." In *The Politics of (M)othering: Womanhood, Identity, and Resistance in African Literature,* edited by Obioma Nnaemeka, 147–61. London and New York: Routledge.

Jackson, C. 1993. "Doing What Comes Naturally? Women and Environment in Development." *World Development* 21 (12): 1947–64.

Jacobs, Susie. 1984. "Women and Land Resettlement in Zimbabwe." *Review of African Political Economy* 27/28: 33–50.

– 1991. "Changing Gender Relations in Zimbabwe: The Case of Individual Family Resettlement Areas." In *Male Bias in the Development Process,* edited by D. Elson, 51–82. Manchester: Manchester University Press.

– 1992. "Gender and Land Reform: Zimbabwe and Some Comparisons." *International Sociology* 7 (1): 5–34.

Jacobs, Susie, and Tracey Howard. 1987. "Women in Zimbabwe: Stated Policy and State Action." In *Women, State, and Ideology: Studies from Africa and Asia,* edited by Haleh Afshar, 28–47. New York: State University of New York Press.

Jayne, T.S., M. Chisvo, and M. Rukuni. 1994. "Zimbabwe's Food Security Paradox: Hunger amid Abundance." In *Zimbabwe's Agricultural Revolution,* edited by M. Rucuni and C.K. Eicher, 289–303. Gweru, Zimbabwe: University of Zimbabwe Publishers; printed by Mambo Press.

Jeater, Diane. 1993. *Marriage, Perversion and Power: The Construction of Moral Discourse in Southern Rhodesia, 1890–1920.* Oxford, Clarendon.

Jiggins, J. 1989. "How Poor Women Earn Income in Sub-Saharan Africa and What Works against Them." *World Development* 17 (7): 953–63.

Jirira, Kwanele Ona. 1995. "Gender, Politics and Democracy: Kuvaka Patsva [Reconstructing] – The Discourse." *Southern African Feminist Review* 1 (2): 1–29.

Joekes, Susan, with Noeleen Heyser, Ruth Oniang'o, and Vania Salles. 1994. "Gender, Environment and Population." *Development and Change* 25 (1): 137–65.

Kadhani, Xavier. 1986. "The Economy: Issues, Problems and Prospects." In *Zimbabwe: The Political Economy of Transition, 1980–86,* edited by Ibbo Mandaza, 99–122. Senegal: CODESRIA (Council for the Development of Social Science Research in Africa).

Kaler, Amy. 2000. "'Who has told you this thing?' Toward a Feminist Interpretation of Contraceptive Diffusion in Rhodesia, 1970–1980." *Signs* 25 (3): 677–708.

Kangai, K., minister of lands and water development, speaking at the Consultative Conference on Land in Zimbabwe, convened by the NGO ZERO, Harare, 28 May 1997.

Keller, Bonnie B. 1978. "Marriage and Medicine: Women's Search for Love and Luck." *African Social Research* 26: 489–505.

Kesby, Mike. 1999. "Locating and Dislocating Gender in Rural Zimbabwe: The Making of Space and the Texturing of Bodies." *Gender, Place and Culture* 6 (1): 27–47.

Kinsey, Bill. 1986. "The Socioeconomics of Nutrition under Stressful Conditions: A Study of Resettlement and Drought in Zimbabwe." Centre for Applied Social Sciences (CASS) Working Paper Series, University of Zimbabwe.

Kriger, N. 1992. *Zimbabwe's Guerilla War: Peasant Voices*. Cambridge: Cambridge University Press.

Lan, David. 1985. *Guns and Rain: Guerrillas and Spirit Mediums in Zimbabwe*. London, Berkeley, and Los Angeles: James Currey and University of California Press.

Landau, Paul. 1995. *The Realm of the Word: Language, Gender and Christianity in a Southern African Kingdom*. Portsmouth, NH: Heinemann.

Larsson, Anita; Matseliso Mapetla; and Ann Schlyter, eds. 1998. *Changing Gender Relations in Southern Africa: Issues of Urban Life*. Roma, Lesotho: Institute of Southern African Studies, National University of Lesotho.

Leach, Melissa. 1994. *Rainforest Relations: Gender and Resource Use among the Mende of Gola, Sierra Leone*. Washington, DC: Smithsonian Institute Press.

Lewis, Desiree. 2000. "SAWPI-A Position Paper." *Southern African Feminist Review* 4 (1): 99–110.

Li, Huey-li. 1993. "A Cross-Cultural Critique of Ecofeminism." In *Ecofeminism: Women, Animals, Nature*, edited by G. Gaard. Philadephia: Temple University Press.

Lindgren, Björn. 2001. "Men Rule, but Blood Speaks: Gender, Identity, and Kingship at the Installation of a Female Chief in Matabeleland, Zimbabwe." In *Changing Men in Southern Africa*, edited by Robert Morrell, 177–94. Pietermaritzburg: University of Natal Press.

Littig, Beate. 2001. *Feminist Perspectives on Environment and Society*. Essex: Pearson Education, Prentice-Hall.

Lopes, Carlos, ed. 1996. *Balancing Rocks: Environment and Development in Zimbabwe*. Harare: Southern African Political Economy Series (SAPES) Publishers.

Maboreke, M. 1991. "Women and Law in Post-Independence Zimbabwe: Experiences and Lessons." In *Putting Women on the Agenda*, edited by Bazilli, 217–47. Johannesburg: Raven Press.

McCulloch, Jock. 2000. *Black Peril, White Virtue: Sexual Crime in Southern Rhodesia, 1902–1935*. Bloomington: Indiana University Press.

McFadden, Patricia. 1996. "Editorial: Sexuality, Identity and Change." *Southern African Feminist Review* 2 (1): vii–ix.

–, ed. 1999. *Reflections on Gender Issues in Africa*. Harare: Southern Africa Political Economy Series (SAPES) Publishers.

– 2002a. "Post-Coloniality in the Zimbabwean Context: Implications for Development Studies." Public lecture, Seminar for National and International Development, Queen's University, Kingston, Ontario, 24 October.

– 2002b. "Becoming Post-Colonial: African Women Change the Meaning of Citizenship." Public lecture, 2002 Robert Sutherland Lecture, Queen's University, Kingston, Ontario, 24 October.

– 2002c. "The Stuggle against Apartheid and Prospects under Post-Colonial Regimes in Southern Africa." Public lecture, Ban Righ Centre, Queen's University, Kingston, Ontario, 25 October.

McGregor, J. 1995. "Conservation, Control and Ecological Change: The Politics and Ecology of Colonial Conservation in Shurugwi, Zimbabwe." *Environment and History* 1(3): 257–80.

MacKenzie, F. 1990. "Gender and Land Rights in Murang'a District, Kenya." *Journal of Peasant Studies* 17 (4): 609–43.

Malahleha, G.M. 1985. "Liquor Brewing: A Cottage Industry in Lesotho Shebeens." *Journal of Eastern African Research and Development* 15:45–55.

Mandishona, G. 1996. "Population Growth Impact in a Sparse Resource Environment." In *Balancing Rocks: Environment and Development in Zimbabwe*, edited by C. Lopes, 33–50. Harare: Southern African Political Economy Series (SAPES) Publishers.

Marongwe, Nelson. 2002. *Conflicts over Land and Other Natural Resources in Zimbabwe*. Harare: ZERO Regional Environment Organisation.

Masoka, Ngoni. 1994. "Land-Reform Policy and Strategy." In *Zimbabwe's Agricultural Revolution*, edited by M. Rukuni and C.K. Eicher, 70–86. Gweru: University of Zimbabwe Publications.

Matowanyika, Joseph Zano Z. 1991. "Indigenous Resource Management and Sustainability in Rural Zimbabwe: An Exploration of Practices and Concepts in Commonlands." Unpublished PhD dissertation, Department of Geography, University of Waterloo, ON.

Maxwell, David. 1999. *Christians and Chiefs in Zimbabwe: A Social History of the Hwesa People c. 1870s–1990s*. London: Edinburgh University Press for the International African Institute.

Meena, R., ed. 1992. *Gender in Southern Africa: Conceptual and Theoretical Issues*. Harare: Southern Africa Political Economy Series (SAPES) Publishers.

Mohanty, Chandra Talpade. 1991. "Under Western Eyes: Feminist Scholarship and Colonial Discourses." In *Third World Women and the Politics of Feminism*, edited by C.T. Mohanty, A. Russo, and L. Torres, 51–80. Bloomington, IN: Indiana University Press.

Moore, David. 2001. "Is the Land the Economy and the Economy the Land? Primitive Accumulation in Zimbabwe." *Journal of Contemporary African Studies* 19 (2): 253–66.

Moore, Donald S. 1993. "Contesting Terrain in Zimbabwe's Eastern Highlands: Political Ecology, Ethnography, and Peasant Resource Struggles." *Economic Geography* 69 (4): 380–401.

Moore, H.L., and M. Vaughn. 1994. *Cutting Down Trees: Gender, Nutrition, and Agricultural Change in the Northern Province of Zambia, 1890–1990*. Portsmouth, NH: Heinemann; London: James Currey; Lusaka: University of Zambia Press.

Morrell, Robert, ed. 1998. *Journal of Southern African Studies* 24 (4). Special issue on Masculinities in Southern Africa.

–, ed. 2001. *Changing Men in Southern Africa*. Pietermaritzburg: University of Natal Press; London and New York: Zed Books.

Mosse, David. 1994. "Authority, Gender and Knowledge: Theoretical Reflections on the Practice of Participatory Rural Appraisal." *Development and Change* 25: 497–525.

Moyana, Henry V. 1984. *The Political Economy of Land in Zimbabwe*. Gweru: Mambo Press.

Moyo, Sam. 1986. "The Land Question." In *Zimbabwe: The Political Eoncomy in Transition, 1980–86*, edited by Ibbo Mandaza, 165–202. Harare: Jongwe Press.

– 1995. "A Gendered Perspective of the Land Question." *Southern African Feminist Review* 1 (1): 13–31.

– 1996. "Land and Democracy in Zimbabwe." Paper presented to the International Conference on the Historical Dimensions of Democracy and Human Rights, University of Zimbabwe, Harare, September.

– 2000. "The Political Economy of Land Acquisition and Redistribution in Zimbabwe, 1990–1999." *Journal of Southern African Studies* 26 (1): 5–28.

Msimang, Sisonke. 2002. "African Feminisms II: Reflections on Politics Made Personal." *Agenda – Empowering Women for Gender Equity* 54:3–15.

Munslow, B. 1985. "Prospects for the Socialist Transition of Agriculture in Zimbabwe." *World Development* 13 (1): 41–58.

Murray, C. 1981. *Families Divided: The Impact of Migrant Labour in Lesotho*. Cambridge: Cambridge University Press.

– 1987. "Class, Gender and the Household: The Developmental Cycle in Southern Africa." *Development and Change* 18:235–49.

Murray, Stephen O., and Will Roscoe, eds. 1998. *Boy-Wives and Female-Husbands: Studies of African Homosexualities*. New York: St Martin's Press.

Mutambirwa, Jane. 1989. "Health Problems in Rural Communities, Zimbabwe." *Social Science Medicine* 29 (8): 927–32.

Mutizwa-Mangiza, N.D., and A.H.J. Helmsing, eds. 1991. *Rural Development and Planning in Zimbabwe*. Aldershot: Avebury.

Ncube, W., and J.E. Stewart et al. 1997. *Paradigms of Exclusion: Women's Access to Resources in Zimbabwe*. Harare: Women and the Law in Southern Africa Research Trust (WLSA).

Nfah-Abbenyi, J.M. 1997. *Gender in African Women's Writing: Identity, Sexuality, and Difference*. Bloomington: Indiana University Press.

Nhira, Calvin, and Louise Fortmann. 1993. "Local Woodland Management: Realities at the Grassroots." In *Living with Trees: Policies for Forestry Management in Zimbabwe*, edited by P. Bradley and K. McNamara, 139–53. Washington, DC: World Bank.

Nkala, Denis. 1996. "Tackling Agricultural Development with Land Dearth." In *Balancing Rocks: Environment and Development in Zimbabwe*, edited by Carlos Lopes, 51–83. Harare: Southern Africa Political Economy Series (SAPES) Publishers.

Nkulukeko, Dabi. 1987. "The Right to Self-Determination in Research: Azanian Women." In *Women in Southern Africa*, edited by C. Qunta, 88–106. London: Allison and Busby.

Nnaemeka, Obioma, ed. 1997. *The Politics of (M)Othering: Womanhood, Identity and Resistance in African Literature*. New York and London: Routledge.

–, ed. 1998. *Sisterhood, Feminisms and Power: From Africa to the Diaspora*. Trenton, NJ: Africa World Press.

Nyambara, Pius S. 2001. "The Closing Frontier: Agrarian Change, Immigrants and the 'Squatter Menace' in Gokwe, 1980s–1990s." *Journal of Agrarian Change* 1 (4): 534–49.

Ong, Aihwa. 1988. "Colonialism and Modernity: Feminist Re- presentations of Women in Non-Western Societies." *Inscriptions* 3 (4): 79–93.

Osirim, Mary Johnson. 2003. "Women, Domestic Violence and Rape in Southern Africa." *African Studies Quarterly* 7 (2&3): (online) <http://web.africa.ufl.edu/asq/v7/v7i2a8.htm>.

Oyewùmí, Oyèrónké. 1997. *The Invention of Women: Making an African Sense of Western Gender Discourses*. Minneapolis: University of Minnesota Press.

Palmer, Robin H. 1977. Land and Racial Domination in Rhodesia. Berkeley and Los Angeles: University of California Press.

Pankhurst, Donna, and Susie Jacobs. 1988. "Land Tenure, Gender Relations, and Agricultural Production: The Case of Zimbabwe's Peasantry." In *Agriculture, Women, and Land: The African Experience*, edited by Jean Davison, 202–27. Boulder and London: Westview Press.

Patai, Daphne. 1991. "U.S. Academics and Third World Women: Is Ethical Research Possible?" In *Women's Words: The Feminist Practice of Oral History*, edited by Sherna Berger Gluck, 137–53. New York: Routledge.

– 1994. "Sick and Tired of Scholars' Nouveau Solipsism." *Chronicle of Higher Education* 40 (25): A52.

Raftopolous, Brian. 2002. "Key Note Address: The Crisis in Zimbabwe." Paper presented at the Canadian Association of African Studies Annual Conference, University of Toronto, Toronto, Ontario, 29 May 2002.

Ranchod-Nilsson, Sita. 1992. "'Educating Eve': The Women's Club Movement and Political Consciousness among Rural African Women in Southern Rhodesia, 1950–1980." In *African Encounters with Domesticity*, edited by K.T. Hansen, 195–217. New Brunswick, NJ: Rutgers University Press.

– 2001. "Warrior Women, Mothers of the Nation, Prostitutes and Traitors: Changing Images of 'the Good Nationalist Woman' in Zimbabwe, 1972–1997." Unpublished paper presented at 2001 Annual Meeting of the International Studies Association, Chicago.

Rangan, Haripriya, and Mary Gilmartin. 2002. "Gender, Traditional Authority, and the Politics of Rural Reform in South Africa." *Development and Change* 33 (4): 633–58.

Ranger, T.O. 1985. *Peasant Consciousness and Guerilla War in Zimbabwe: A Comparative Study.* London: J. Currey; Berkeley: University of California Press.

– 1993. "The Local and the Global in Southern African Religious History." In *Conversion to Christianity: Historical and Anthropological Persepctives on a Great Transformation*, edited by Robert W. Hefner, 65–98. Berkeley, Los Angeles, and Oxford: University of California Press.

Razavi, Shahra, ed. 2002."Introduction." In *Shifting Burders: Gender and Agrarian Change under Neoliberalism*, 1–34. Bloomfield, CT: Kumarian Press.

Rhodesia. 1973. *Agricultural Development Authority: Annual Report and Accounts.* Salisbury.

Robins, Steven. 2003. "Whose Modernity? Indigenous Modernities and Land Claims after Apartheid." *Development and Change* 34 (2): 265–85.

Rocheleau, Diane; B. Thomas-Slayter; and Ester Wangari, eds. 1996. *Feminist Political Ecology: Global Issues and Local Experiences.* London and New York: Routledge.

Rukuni, M. 1994. *Report on the Inquiry into Appropriate Agricultural Land Tenure Systems* ("The Rukuni Report"). Executive Summary for His Excellency the President of the Republic of Zimbabwe, vol. 1: Main Report; vol. 2: Technical Reports. Harare: Government Printers.

Rukuni, M., and C.K. Eicher, eds. 1994. *Zimbabwe's Agricultural Revolution.* Gweru: University of Zimbabwe Publications.

Runganga, A.; M. Pitts; and J. McMaster. 1992. "The Use of Herbal and Other Agents to Enhance Sexual Experience." *Social Science and Medicine* 35 (8): 1037–42.

Rutherford, Blair. 2001a. "Commercial Farm Workers and the Politics of (Dis)placement in Zimbabwe: Colonialism. Liberation and Democracy." *Journal of Agrarian Change* 1 (4): 626–51.

– 2001b. *Working on the Margins: Black Workers, White Farmers in Postcolonial Zimbabwe*. London and New York: Zed Books.

Sachikonye, Lloyd M. 2003. *The Situation of Commercial Farm Workers after Land Reform in Zimbabwe: A Report Prepared for the Farm Community Trust of Zimbabwe*. March.

Sachs, Carolyn E., ed. 1997. *Women Working the Environment*. Washington, DC: Taylor and Francis.

Sahlins, M. 1999. "What Is Anthropological Enlightenment? Some Lessons of the Twentieth Century." *Annual Review of Anthropology* 28:i–xxiii.

Salleh, Ariel. 1997. *Ecofeminism as Politics: Nature, Marx and the Postmodern*. London and New York: Zed Books.

Schmidt, E. 1992a. *Peasants, Traders and Wives: Shona Women in the History of Zimbabwe, 1870–1939*. Portsmouth, NH: Heinemann.

– 1992b. "Race, Sex, and Domestic Labour: The Question of African Female Servants in Southern Rhodesia, 1900–1939." In *African Encounters with Domesticity*, edited by K. Hansen, 221–41. New Brunswick, NJ: Rutgers University Press.

Schoffeleers, J.M. 1979. *Guardians of the Land: Essays on Central African Territorial Cults*. Gwelo, Zimbabwe: Mambo Press.

Schroeder, Richard A. 2001. "'Gone to Their Second Husbands': Marital Metaphors and Conjugal Contracts in the Gambia's Female Garden Sector." In *"Wicked" Women and the Reconfiguration of Gender in Africa*, edited by D.L. Hodgson and S.A. McCurdy, 85–105. Portsmouth, NJ: Heinemann.

Scoones, Ian, and John Thompson, eds. 1994. *Beyond Farmer First: Rural People's Knowledge, Agricultural Research and Extension Practice*. London: Intermediate Technology Publications, International Institute for Environment and Development.

Shiripinda, Iris. 2000. "Legislative Aspects in Relation to HIV/AIDS Prevention in Zimbabwe." *Southern African Feminist Review* 4 (1): 37–44.

Shiva, Vandana. 1988. *Staying Alive: Women, Ecology and Development*. London and New York: Zed Books.

Shiva, Vandana, and Maria Mies. 1993. *Ecofeminism*. London: Zed Books.

Shutt, Allison Kim. 1995. *"We are the best poor farmers": Purchase Area Farmers and Economic Differentiation in Southern Rhodesia, c. 1925–1980*. Unpublished PhD dissertation, University of California.

Sithole, Bev. 1997. "The institutional framework for the management and use of natural resources in communal areas of Zimbabwe: Village cases of access to and use of dambos from Mutoko and Chiduku." Monograph, Centre for Applied Social Sciences (CASS), University of Zimbabwe.

Southern African Feminist Review (SAFERE) 4 (1). 2000. "Zimbabwean Women Engage with the Constitution," 47–95.

Southern Rhodesia. 1944. *Report of Native Production and Trade Commission.* Salisbury.

– 1952. "Native Land Husbandry Act 1951". The Statutes of Law of Southern Rhodesia 1951. Acts of Parliament January to December: 893–922.

Speak Out/Tauria/Khulumani, no. 33. 1995.

Stewart, Julie. 1992. "Inheritance in Zimbabwe: The Quiet Revolution." In *Working Papers on Inheritance in Zimbabwe,* edited by J. Stewart. Women and the Law in Southern Africa Research Project. Working Paper No. 5, Harare.

Stewart, Julie, et al. 2000. *In the Shadow of the Law: Women and Justice Delivery in Zimbabwe.* Harare: Women and Law in Southern Africa Research Trust (WLSA).

Stewart, Julie; W. Ncube; M. Maboreke; and A. Armstrong. 1990. "The Legal Situation of Women in Zimbabwe." In *The Legal Situation of Women in Southern Africa,* edited by J. Stewart and A. Armstrong, 165–222. Harare: University of Zimbabwe Publications.

Stoneman, C., ed. 1988. *Zimbabwe's Prospects: Issues of Race, Class, State and Capital in Southern Africa.* Basingstoke: Macmillan.

Sturgeon, Noel. 1997. *Ecofeminist Natures: Race, Gender, Feminist Theory and Political Action.* New York and London: Routledge.

Sylvester, Christine. 1995. "'Women' in Rural Producer Groups and the Diverse Politics of Truth in Zimbabwe." In *Feminism/Postmodernism/Development,* edited by J. Parpart and M. Marchand, 182–203. London: Routledge.

– 2000. *Producing Women and Progress in Zimbabwe: Narratives of Identity and Work from the 1980s.* Portsmouth, NH: Heinemann.

Thomas-Slayter, B.; Wangari, E.; and D. Rocheleau. 1996. "Feminist Political Ecology." In *Feminist Political Ecology: Global Issues and Local Experiences,* edited by Diane Rocheleau, B. Thomas-Slayter, and Ester Wangari, 287–307. London and New York: Routledge.

Thompson, Guy. 2002. "We Were Like Reeled Fish: Peasant Constructions of Historical Change in Zimbabwe." Paper presented at the Canadian Association for African Studies annual conference, University of Toronto, 29 May 2002.

UNAIDS. 2002. "Report on the Global HIV/AIDS Epidemic, July 2002" <http://www.unaids.org/barcelona/presskitbarcelona%20report/table.pdf>.

Vivian, Jessica. 1994. "NGOs and Sustainable Development in Zimbabwe: No Magic Bullets." *Development and Change* 25:167–93.

Walker, Cherryl. 2002. "Land Reform and the Empowerment of Rural Women in Postapartheid South Africa." In *Shifting Burdens: Gender and Agrarian Change under Neoliberalism*, edited by Shahra Razavi, 67–92. Bloomfield, CT: Kumarian Press.

Wanzala, Winnie. 1998. "Towards an Epistemological and Methodological Framework." In *Gender in Southern Africa: A Gendered Perspective*, edited by P. McFadden, 1–26. Harare: Southern Africa Political Economy Series (SAPES) Books.

Weiner, D. 1988. "Land and Agricultural Development." In *Zimbabwe's Prospects: Issues of Race, Class, State and Capital in Southern Africa*, edited by C. Stoneman, 63–89. Macmillan.

Weinrich, A. 1979. *Women and Racial Discrimination in Rhodesia*. Paris: UNESCO.

Wekwete, K.H. 1991. "The Rural Resettlement Programme in Post-Independence Zimbabwe." In *Rural Development and Planning in Zimbabwe*, edited by N.D. Mutizwa-Mangiza and A.H.J. Helmsing, 113–42. Aldershot: Avebury.

Wilson, K.B. 1989. "Trees in Fields in Southern Africa." *Journal of Southern African Studies* 15:369–83.

– 1995. "'Water Used to be Scattered in the Landscape': Local Understandings of Soil Erosion and Land Use Planning in Southern Zimbabwe." *Environment and History* 1 (3): 281–96.

With These Hands: How Women Feed Africa. 1986. Documentary film. Producted by New Internationalist; distributed by Full Frame Film & Video.

Wolf, Diane. 1996. "Situating Feminist Dilemmas in Fieldwork." In *Feminist Dilemmas in Fieldwork*, edited by D. Wolf, 1–25. Boulder: Westview Press.

Women and Land Lobby Group (WLLG). 2000. "Women's Land Rights in Southern Africa." Proceedings from a regional conference hosted by WLLG and Friedrich-Ebert-Stiftung, Sheraton Hotel, Harare, 27–28 November 2000.

– 2001a. "Report on the Workshop Organized by the Ministry of Youth, Gender and Employment Creation and the Women and Land Lobby Group on Gender Gaps in Land Reform Policy Documents." Proceedings from workshop held at the Bronte Hotel, Harare, 22 May 2001.

– 2001b. "Urban Agriculture and the Role of the Women and Land Lobby Group in Zimbabwe." <http://www.ruaf.org/no4/18_wo_zim.htm>.

Worby, Eric. 2001. "A Redivided Land? New Agrarian Conflicts and Questions in Zimbabwe." *Journal of Agrarian Change* 1 (4): 475–509.

World Bank. 1985. "Zimbabwe Land Subsector Study." Washington, DC.

Zimbabwe. 1982. *Transitional National Development Plan 1982/83–1984/85*. Vol. 1. Harare: Government Printers.

– 1986. *First Five-Year National Development Plan 1986–91*. Vol. 1. Harare: Government Printers.

– 1988. *First Five-Year National Development Plan 1986–91*. Vol. 2. Harare: Government Printers.

– 1991. *Second Five-Year National Development Plan 1991–1995*. Harare: Government Printers.

– 1993. *Policies and Procedures: Resettlement and the Reorganization of Communal Lands*. Ministry of Local Government, Rural and Urban Development, Harare.

– 1998. *Land Reform and Resettlement Program: Phase II 1998*. Ministry of Lands, Agriculture and Rural Resettlement.

– 1999. *Inception Phase Framework Plan, 1999–2000: An Implementation Plan of the Land Reform and Resettlement Programme – Phase 2*. Prepared by the Technical Committee on Resettlement and Rural Development and National Economic Consultative Forum on Land Task Force.

– 2000. *The Accelerated Land Reform and Resettlement Implementation Plan (Fast Track) 2000*. Ministry of Lands, Agriculture and Rural Resettlement.

– 2001. *Land Reform and Resettlement Programme: Revised Phase II*. Ministry of Lands, Agriculture and Rural Resettlement. April.

Zimbabwe-Rhodesia. 1979. *Integrated Plan for Rural Development July 1978*. Ministry of Finance, Salisbury.

Zimbabwe Women's Resource Centre and Network (ZWRCN). 1994a. "The Gender Dimension of Access and Land Use Rights in Zimbabwe: Evidence to the Land Commission." Harare: ZWRCN.

– 1994b. *Impact of Interaction between Men and Women on Women and Development in Zimbabwe. Culture Survey*. Harare: ZWRCN.

– 1995. *Zimbabwe Women's Voices*. Harare: ZWRCN.

– 1996. *Woman Plus*. Special issue: *Women and Land*. Harare: ZWRCN.

Zinanga, Evelyn. 1996. "Sexuality and the Heterosexual Form: The Case of Zimbabwe." *Southern African Feminist Review* 2 (1): 3–6.

Zinyama, L.M. 1991. "Agricultural Development Policies in the African Farming Areas of Zimbabwe." In *Rural Development and Planning in Zimbabwe*, edited by N.D. Mutizwa-Mangiza and A.H.J. Helmsing, 95–142. Aldershot: Avebury.

Index